whales, candlelight, and *stuff* like that

Whales, Candlelight, and *Stuff* Like That

GENERAL EXTENDERS IN
ENGLISH DISCOURSE

Maryann Overstreet

New York   Oxford
Oxford University Press
1999

Oxford University Press

Oxford   New York

Athens   Auckland   Bangkok   Bogotá   Buenos Aires   Calcutta
Cape Town   Chennai   Dar es Salaam   Delhi   Florence   Hong Kong   Istanbul
Karachi   Kuala Lumpur   Madrid   Melbourne   Mexico City   Mumbai
Nairobi   Paris   São Paulo   Singapore   Taipei   Tokyo   Toronto   Warsaw

and associated companies in
Berlin   Ibadan

Copyright © 1999 by Maryann Overstreet

Published by Oxford University Press, Inc.
198 Madison Avenue, New York, New York 10016

Oxford is a registered trademark of Oxford University Press.

Library of Congress Cataloging-in-Publication Data
Overstreet, Maryann, 1962–
Whales, candlelight, and stuff like that : general extenders in English discourse / Maryann Overstreet.
p.   cm.
Includes bibliographical references and index.
ISBN 0-19-512574-6
1. English language—Discourse analysis.   2. English language—Spoken English.
3. Interpersonal communication.   4. Speech acts (Linguistics)   5. Conversation analysis.
6. Pragmatics.   I. Title.
PE1422.094   1999
420.1'41—dc21   98-45489

1 3 5 7 9 8 6 4 2

Printed in the United States of America
on acid-free paper

For George

Acknowledgments

First, I would like to thank George Yule, without whose generous guidance and support this book would never have been written.

I am grateful to Jack Bilmes, for introducing me to the study of conversation, and for first bringing the phenomenon of general extenders to my attention.

I am indebted to my friends and family, who allowed me to record their conversations and analyze them. I am especially grateful to Erin Britos, Suzy Byrd, Debbie DuBois, Shirley and Randy Hurst, John Jensen, Cathy Overstreet Ritter, Fred Overstreet, Jean Overstreet, Dennis Revuelto, Tana Trantham, Jimmy Williams, and Maghna Zettle.

I would also like to thank the following individuals for reading earlier drafts of this work and providing helpful comments: George Grace, Cornelia Moore, Ken Rehg, and Al Schütz. For words of encouragement I'm grateful to Alice Bertschinger, Hugh Buckingham, Cynthia Clement, Margaret Early, Katinka Hammerich, Elaine Hatfield, Gabi Kasper, Louise Kidd, Eric Kellerman, Todd Masuda, Dick Rapson, Elaine Tarone, Ruth Weisel, David Williams, and Ann Yule.

Special thanks to Peter Ohlin and MaryBeth Branigan of Oxford University Press for their editorial assistance.

Many other individuals have contributed to this work in various ways. I am grateful to Terrie Mathis for some wonderful data. Other excellent examples were found in data collected by Anna Guthrie (1994). For help with examples from other languages I am indebted to: Haruko Cook, Yumiko Ohara, and Scott Saft (Japanese), Niklaus Schweizer (Hawaiian), and Sang-Sup Kim (Korean). Liz Nakoa assisted in the creation of computerized drawings, and Ray Moody and Shiel Yule provided technical advice. Finally, Kula Overstreet provided constant companionship, and, at times, welcome distraction.

Contents

Part Four: Conclusion

Transcription Conventions

.	A period indicates a stopping fall in tone.
,	A comma indicates continuing intonation.
!	An exclamation point indicates an animated tone.
?	A question mark indicates a rising tone.
:	A colon indicates a lengthened segment.
_ _	Underlining indicates stress (loudness).
CAP	Capital letters indicate extreme stress (loudness).
(.5)	Indicates the length of a pause in seconds.
(( ))	Double parentheses contain a description by the transcriptionist.
( )	Single parentheses mark transcribed material which is in doubt (i.e., the transcriptionist is not certain what was said).
(*)	Each asterisk between single parentheses represents approximately one-half second of material which is in doubt.
.hh	Audible inhalation
hh	Audible exhalation
//	Indicates the point at which the next speaker begins to speak (in overlap). For example, in [1], Maya's utterance begins in the middle of Sara's 'now':

[1] 1. Sara: I think they must have broke up or
          something 'cause he's back no//w.
     2. Maya: Yeah, they must've.

= When there is no interval between adjacent utterances, the two utterances are linked together with equal signs. For example, in turn 2 of [2], Blake's 'Wait' is immediately followed by Donna's 'Your . . .' in turn 3; Donna's 'here' in turn 3 is then immediately followed by Blake's 'He . . .' in turn 4.

[2] 1. Donna: So what was I just—Oh. So Henry and I were talking last night an' he was saying 'I can ne:ver—(.) I::' Here's what he did. This is his hand motions. He goes

   2. Blake: Wait.=

   3. Donna: ='Your intelligence level is up he::re, and I am down he::re.'=

   4. Blake: =He said that?

This symbol may also indicate a lack of pause within one person's turn, where a pause might be expected. For example, in [3], there is no pause between Sara's utterance of 'day' and 'y'know':

[3] Sara: Lemme ask you thi::s .hh this is just somethin' that dawned on me the other day=y'know in Louisiana it's kinda hard to open a bank account without a Louisiana driver's license . . .

Ø Indicates a 'zero quotative' (see Mathis 1992; Mathis and Yule 1994). This occurs in reported speech and marks a shift in speakers where the shift is not overtly marked by a quotative phrase, such as 'she said' or 'she's like.' For example, in [4], there is a shift in speakers in line 2, between the utterances 'Why—Why did—' and 'I'm not gonna go with Sara because .hh you're upset with—.'

[4] Maya: . . . she comes over an' she's like '(h)I—I ran over here' an' I'm like 'Why? Why did—' Ø 'I'm not gonna go with Sara because .hh you're upset with—' I'm like 'No, I'm not upset with you. I'm over it.'

PART ONE

Preliminaries

–1–

Introduction

Did you wanna go look at some shoes and stuff, or something, or what?

During the spring of 1995, I was visiting an aunt in Birmingham, Alabama. We were leaving a restaurant in a shopping mall after lunch, and discussing what we would do that afternoon, when my aunt produced the question that is quoted above. I'm not sure if I ever answered that question, nor do I recall going to look at shoes. But I do remember the utterance. It contains three versions of a type of expression I had been studying for some time. They are *and stuff, or something,* and *or what.* Displaying great virtuosity in the use of these forms, my aunt had given voice to the problematic nature of the moment for a woman wondering what to do next with a visitor whose interests she barely knew.

General Extenders

The goal of this book is to describe and offer an analysis not just of the forms my aunt used but of a whole range of such expressions. They represent a distinct set of linguistic elements which have received little attention from linguists but are clearly important for users of language. These expressions, which are pervasive in ordinary conversation, serve a number of functions which vary according to contexts of use.

The forms to be described and analyzed constitute a class of expressions that typically occur in clause-final position and have the basic form of conjunction plus noun phrase. I call these expressions "general extenders": "general" because they are nonspecific, and "extenders" because they extend otherwise grammatically complete utterances. They can be divided into two sets: those beginning with

3

and (*and stuff, and everything*), which will be called "adjunctive general extenders," and those beginning with *or* (*or something, or anything*), which will be called "disjunctive general extenders." An idea of the range of possible types of expressions that could be classified as general extenders is provided in the following list.

and stuff (like that)	or something (like that)
and all (that)	or anything (like that)
and everything (like that)	or what
and blah blah blah	or whatever
and that	or what have you
and the like	or anyone (like that)
and such	or anybody (like that)
and what have you	or someone (like that)
and so on	or somebody (like that)
and so forth	or someplace (like that)
and whatnot	or somewhere (like that)
and the rest	
and this and that	
and whatever	
and you name it	
and the whole kit and caboodle	
and the whole nine yards	
and the whole bit/thing	
and (all) {this/that}	

and (all) {this/that} {sort/kind/type} of
    {crap/thing/jazz/junk/mess/nonsense/shit/stuff}
and {crap/things/junk/shit/stuff} (like this/that)
and {business/crap/things/junk/shit} of {this/that}
    {kind/sort/ilk/nature}
et cetera

This list is not exhaustive. Variations on these forms, and more novel creations, are not infrequent.

Contexts of Occurrence

I have been collecting and attempting to analyze examples of general extenders for several years. Once I started listening for them, I heard them in every possible context. In the chapters that follow, I will present many examples transcribed from recorded conversational data. I will also include a number of examples that I have found in a wide range of other contexts. As illustrated below, general extenders can occur [1] in a spoken narrative, [2] in a newspaper article, [3] in the lyrics of a song, [4] at an airline check-in counter, [5] in a stand-up comedy routine, [6] during a space walk, [7] in a telephone answering machine message, [8] in an interview, [9] in an emergency (911) phone call, or [10] on news radio.

[1]   S: One time. back in the seventies. when I was married ta Jim. an' there was a sugar shortage an' a-like he sold pot **'n stuff** . . . (Guthrie 1994: 59)

[2]   (Quote about Nolan Ryan, the pitcher)
      "The Lord uniquely put those hinges together and the elbow and the musculature **and all that kind of stuff** to make him be able to throw the ball as hard as he did for as long as he did," Toborg said. (*Honolulu Star-Bulletin*, 24 Sept. 1993)

[3]   (From *John Brown*, by Bob Dylan)
      John Brown went off to war to fight on a foreign shore.
      His mama sure was proud of him!
      He stood straight and tall in his uniform **and all**.

[4]   (Group leader to group members in line)
      Leader: Make sure your bag has a tag with your name and address **and everything**.

[5]   (From *Richard Pryor Live in Concert*)
      People try to be macho ma::::n. That'll get you fucked up, Jack. Especially nowadays, 'cause young dudes that fight they don't even fight like (.) older people you know what I mean like we used to just have gang fights and you'd use your fists **an' shit**=Now they've got that Kung Fu and Karate **an' shit**=they'd like to pluck your eye out and pull your arm outta socket **an' shit**.

[6]   (The first untethered space walk, 7 Feb. 1984)
      Captain McCandless: I show myself about eighty feet out, **something like that**. I could go faster, but why rush it? . . .

Are you going to want the windows washed **or something**
while I'm up here? (Stevenson 1987: 330)

[7]   (Jeremy is one of Roger's students)
       Roger, it's Jeremy. I heard—I heard—(*) well, I came to
       class but they have a (.5) bomb threat **or something**. .hhh
       Wow, some guys will do anything to get out of class. No. I
       just wanted to let you know that um I—I tried to make it
       today and wanted to make it but I—I wasn't ducking out
       or anything . . .

[8]   (An interview with Noam Chomsky)
       Chomsky: That's the kind of work you would hope would
       soon be done: to take a theory of universal grammar, fix the
       parameters one way or another, and then deduce from these
       parameters the grammar of a real human language—
       Japanese, Swahili, English, **or whatnot**. (Gliedman 1983:
       171)

[9]   (Excerpts from 911 records appearing in article on
       O.J. Simpson case)
       911 Operator: Is he the sportscaster **or whatever**?
       Nicole: Yes. Thank you.   (Turque et al. 1994: 24)

[10]   (A discussion of life in 1930s America)
       . . . some (.) young women said as long as they didn't take
       money u:h they were not prostitutes- as long as they took
       gifts, um foo::d, clo:thing, **et cetera** . . . (National Public
       Radio, Feb. 1995)

These examples and most of those used to illustrate points throughout
the following chapters are from contemporary spoken and written
English. I have not attempted a historical investigation of these
forms. However, I have noted, and included later, an example from
Jane Austen's *Persuasion* (1818) and two of many examples in J. D.
Salinger's *The Catcher in the Rye* (1951).[1] There is little doubt that
general extenders have been part of the English language for many
years.

     Although general extenders are found in both spoken and written
contexts, the frequency of these forms appears to be highest in informal, spoken conversation among familiars.[2] For example, in my corpus
of ten hours of recorded telephone conversations and face-to-face
interactions among familiars, there were 156 occurrences of general
extenders. In contrast, in ten hours of recorded spoken interaction
among nonfamiliars in formal settings (e.g., news radio interviews,

political debates, academic discussions, and courtroom deliberations), I found just thirty occurrences of general extenders.

Table 1.1 illustrates the occurrence of different forms in these two databases.

Table 1.1   Distribution of General Extenders

Forms	Informal Spoken	Formal Spoken
and stuff	29	0
and everything	12	0
and blah blah blah	4	0
and all that stuff	4	0
and all	3	0
and things like that	3	1
and all this stuff	2	0
and that kind of thing	2	0
and whatever	2	0
and so on	0	8
et cetera	0	7
and all that	1	4
and so forth	0	3
or something	42	3
or something like that	4	0
or what	4	0
or whatever	16	0
or anything	19	0
or somewhere	2	0
Total adjunctive	67	27
Total disjunctive	89	3
Total*	156	30

*Forms that occurred only once are not listed in the table. These include *and things, and all that shit, and all that crap, and that kind of stuff, and whatnot, or anything like that,* and *or something or other* (in the "informal" corpus); and *and things of that sort, and all this,* and *so on=and so forth,* and *et cetera=et cetera* (in the "formal" corpus).

The following observations can be made on the basis of this data:

1. Certain forms are found primarily in informal spoken contexts
    and talk among familiars (e.g., *or anything, and everything,
    and stuff, and blah blah blah*), whereas other forms are found
    primarily in formal spoken contexts and talk among
    nonfamiliars (e.g., *et cetera, and so on, and so forth*).
2. Although certain forms are found primarily in one of the two
    contexts described above, other forms occur in both (e.g., *and
    things like that, and all this/that, or something*).
3. Disjunctive general extenders occur much more frequently in
    informal spoken contexts and talk among familiars (89 of 156,
    or 57 percent of the total number of occurrences) than in
    formal spoken contexts and talk among nonfamiliars (3 of 30,
    or 10 percent of the total number of occurrences).

The occurrence of general extenders has been noted in many varieties of English, including Australian (Dines 1980), English (Aijmer 1985, Channell 1994), Scottish (Macaulay 1985, 1991), and American (Ball and Ariel 1978, Jefferson 1990), and in many other languages, as well. The following are examples from Swedish [11], Dutch [12], German [13], French [14], Spanish [15], Japanese [16], Korean [17], and Hawaiian [18].[3]

[11] *Vi satt å prata å så där*
      We sat and talked **and that**
      (Aijmer 1985: 389)

[12] Patient: *En zondagavond kree'k eh pijn in m'n borst hier*
      And Sunday night I got uh pain in my chest here
      Doctor: *Met hoesten of zo of nou—*
      With coughing **or something or whatever**—
      (Have 1991: 144)

[13] (Magazine interview with a professional swimmer)
      Stern: *Gehen Sie gern zu solchen Anlässen?*
      Do you like going to such occasions?
      Völker: *Kommt drauf an. Manchmal ist mir das ein bißchen
      peinlich, weil ich immer noch nicht richtig tanzen kann—
      Walzer **und so**.*
      It depends. Sometimes I find it embarrassing, because
      I still can't dance well—waltzes **and such**. (*Stern* 21 May
      1995)

[14] *Je jouais au hockey pour le collège, au hockey-salon au: au hockey intérieur tu sais des affaires de même tu sais, des activités parascolaires là.*
I played hockey for the college, floor-hockey, inside hockey, you know, **things like that** you know, extracurricular activities.   (DuBois 1993: 180)

[15] *. . . hasta que, no más dije—Iy, heart attack o algo.*
until, I [simply] said, "Oh, a heart attack **or something**,"
(Koike 1996: 278)

[16] (Apartment description)
. . . ++ de basu-ruumu wa syawaa to ANO nagasiba to otearai ga atte AA nante iun desu ka monoire ga ne sukosi konogurai no haba no doa to ++ hukasa ga konogurai no monoire ga arimasu ne + ano ima iroiro ++ sono basu-ruumu de tukau mono taoru to ka ne ato ++ otearai no kami to ka sekken to ka sonna mono o irete irun desu keredomo ANO yuka kara zutto ue made ++ tenzyoo made no ookina monoire kanari hairimasu kedo ne.
. . . And the bathroom has a shower, a sink, and a toilet. And what do you call it? a closet, with, I wonder how much, about this width of a door and this much depth, we have this closet. We put in stuff we use, towel, toilet paper, and soap, **and things like that, that kind of stuff**. It is from the floor to the ceiling. It's a big closet. You can put a lot in it. (Hatch 1992: 177)

[17] *Namsanpun anira pukhansan, dobongsan deung Seoul inkuneu saneneun modu ireun sankoyangyidulyi deuksilkurinda.*
Wild cats crowd such Seoul mountains as Nam-San, Puk-Han-San, Do-Bong-San **and so on**.   (Lee 1998: 28)

[18] *"Ike ia Kaleponi, he aina anu, a pela aku."*
"Look at California, it is a cold place, **and so forth**."
(McGuire 1938: 11)

It should be emphasized that while general extenders are found in many different languages and contexts, this investigation will focus primarily on forms found in one corpus of American English data, which consists of informal, spoken interactions among familiars. This database and the rationale for this approach are described in further detail in the last section of this chapter.

A Note on Grammatical Agreement

In many ways, general extenders do not seem to be constrained by strict grammatical agreement requirements. As illustrated below, syntactic category differences between the conjuncts [19]–[22], can be observed, as can number differences [23] and gender differences [24].

[19] (VP *and* NP)
      she's sort of a child who swings and does somersaults **and stuff like that** (Dines 1980: 28)

[20] (AdjP *and* NP)
      . . . they just think, maybe you're kooky **or something**
      (Ball and Ariel 1978: 37–8)

[21] (S *or* NP)[4]
      They forgot to bring the leftovers, or they didn't have time, **or something**. (Ball and Ariel 1978: 38)

[22] (PP *or* NP)
      Everybody I know wants some kind of soft parts rubbed up against their soft parts. Or in their facial area **or something**.

[23] (plural count *and* non-count)
      Yeah. Most of 'em are evergreens around there I guess. Pine trees **and stuff**.

[24] (feminine *or* neuter)
      At the risk of sounding like Miss America **or something**, I wanted to do something to help. (HIV-positive man undergoing experimental gene therapy, interviewed on CNN, 3 July 1996)

The fact that a general extender can be coordinated with a variety of conjuncts often makes it difficult to determine exactly which part of the preceding utterance it is conjoined with. For example, in [19], my personal impression is that the conjunction involves *swings* (VP) and *does somersaults* (VP) *and stuff like that* (NP). However, it is possible to view the conjunction as only involving *somersaults* (NP) *and stuff like that* (NP). Other alternatives would be that the form *or something* in [20] is coordinated with the VP *are kooky*, and that *or something* in [22] is coordinated with the NP *facial area*. As Aijmer (1985) and Channell (1994) have noted, these ambiguities can sometimes be resolved in speech, where intonation may help to identify which element the general extender is coordinated with. In general, however, paralinguistic clues such as intonation are not a consistently reliable guide in this type of analysis.

Although I have characterized the two types of general extenders as adjunctive (*and. . .*) and disjunctive (*or. . .*), on the basis of the conjunctions used, there are occasions when the actual conjunctions are missing. As already shown in example [6], the phrase *something like that*, repeated here as [25], occurs without *or*; also, in [26], the form *blah blah blah* is used without *and*.

[25]   I show myself about eighty feet out, **something like that.**

[26]   it's just about, you know, questions like, you know, are you still coming the twelfth, do you need me to meet you somewhere, **blah blah blah.**

I have not attempted to analyze the circumstances in which this type of elision takes place, but it is sufficiently infrequent in the primary database under investigation that I leave this issue for future study and concentrate here on the analysis of the more frequent constructions with conjunctions.

Function

The widespread use of general extenders suggests that these expressions are indeed important for language users. But what functions do they serve? In previous research, the focus has been on finding a referential meaning for these forms.[5] For example, general extenders have been analyzed as list completers (Jefferson 1990, Lerner 1994), set-marking tags (Dines 1980, Ward and Birner 1993), and vague category identifiers (Channell 1994). In most cases, the general extender has been treated as a form that indicates additional members of a list, set, or category. The general assumption has been that these expressions combine with a named exemplar (or exemplars), whose characteristics make it possible for the hearer to infer a category the speaker has in mind. Following this approach, an expression such as *apples and stuff* might be analyzed as having the same referent as the category *fruit*. Interestingly, little consideration has been given to how this process of inference might work on a particular occasion, or to why a speaker might choose to use such a non-specific form of reference.

In contrast, I hope to show that general extenders are best viewed as multifunctional forms which do not serve a predominantly referential function, but rather have a much more interpersonally defined role. Rather than having list completion or set-marking as their primary function, these expressions are used by speakers to indicate assumptions of shared knowledge and experience, or to mark an attitude toward the message expressed, or toward the hearer. The function performed by a general extender on a given occasion is likely to be strongly determined by the speaker–hearer context of occurrence, as well as by the type of utterance (e.g., invitation, offer, suggestion, or assertion) in which it occurs.

As a consequence, I have avoided using any version of the type of analytic terminology that has been used in previous studies to label these expressions in terms of a single, referential function. I do not call these forms "generalized list completers" (Jefferson 1990, Lerner 1994) because, as argued in chapter 2, list completion clearly is not their primary or sole function. Similarly, I avoid calling these expressions "set-marking tags" (Dines 1980, Ward and Birner 1993), or "vague category identifiers" (Channell 1994). As demonstrated in chapters 3 and 4, it is misleading to assume that these forms function simply to indicate other members of a category or set. I am not alone in this view. Early on, Ball and Ariel (1978) noted that people did not simply interpret *or something* on the basis of set-marking. In another study, Macaulay (1985) commented on the fact that many examples in his data were difficult to analyze as marking any kind of set. A broader analysis and more open term clearly are required. I have found the term "general extender" to be appropriately neutral with regard to possible competing functions (list-completing, set-marking, or whatever). It also provides a simple analytic contrast between "general extenders" (e.g., *and all that stuff*) and what might be called "specific extenders" (e.g., *and all of that stupid bureaucratic stuff*), in which there is more specific lexical material used within the phrase.

Given their apparent discourse function, it might be possible to describe general extenders as types of "discourse markers" related functionally to expressions such as *you know* and *I mean*, as described in Schiffrin (1987). In fact, the close co-occurrence of *you know* (illustrated in chapter 5) and *I mean* (shown in chapter 6) with general extenders suggests that there is some connection or shared function among these forms. Like these discourse markers, general extenders function on an interpersonal level and can reflect the speaker's attitude toward the message or addressee. However, general extenders differ from discourse markers in several notable ways. Whereas discourse markers represent a disparate list of items, belonging to different word classes (Schiffrin 1987: 40), general extenders are a relatively homogeneous set of forms consisting of a conjunction (*and* or *or*) plus a noun phrase. Unlike discourse markers, which function parenthetically and are independent of sentence structure, general extenders are syntactically conjoined to utterances and thus part of sentence structure. Finally, whereas several discourse markers (*you know, I mean, oh, like*) "can occur quite freely within a sentence at locations which are very difficult to define syntactically"

(Schiffrin 1987: 32), general extenders typically occur in clause-final position. (There appears to be some evidence, however, that certain forms, such as *and stuff*, may be in the process of becoming more flexible with regard to position; this will be discussed in chapter 7.)

With these factors in mind, general extenders may be more appropriately classified, along with discourse markers, as members of a much larger class of forms known as "pragmatic operators." Indeed, Ariel (1994: 3250) lists the form *or something*, along with discourse markers, as a member of this class. The entire group of general extenders appears to fit the definition of pragmatic operators as forms that "convey metalinguistic messages concerning either speaker-utterance, addressee-utterance, utterance-utterance relations, or else they constitute an interpersonal communication between speaker and addressee" (Ariel 1994: 3250). Whether they will eventually be classified as clear instances of pragmatic operators, or simply as types of the much larger group termed "pragmatic expressions" (Östman 1981), general extenders deserve to be analyzed at this stage as a group of related expressions important in their own right. They are connected to, but certainly not identical to, the other, more commonly studied examples of discourse markers and pragmatic devices.

Analytic Approach

The analysis of general extenders presented in this study is undertaken within that general approach to the study of language known as discourse analysis, as exemplified in the work of Brown and Yule (1983a) and Tannen (1989). This analytic approach has certain crucial elements, identified in this definition by Brown and Yule:

> The analysis of discourse is, necessarily, the analysis of language in use. As such, it cannot be restricted to the description of linguistic forms independent of the purposes or functions which these forms are designed to serve in human affairs. While some linguists may concentrate on determining the formal properties of a language, the discourse analyst is committed to an investigation of what that language is used for. (1983a: 1)

Note that the term "discourse analysis" does not refer to any single theory or method employed in the study of language in use. Rather, it represents a broad range of theories and methods with one thing in common: the analysis of language beyond the sentence level. Tannen suggests that these diverse theories and methods have been grouped together under one term in order to:

make legitimate types of analysis of types of language
that do not fit into the established subfields of linguistics,
more narrowly focused, which had come to be regarded by
many as synonymous with the name of the discipline, and
to encompass work in other disciplines that also study language. Some of the work of Jakobson, Sapir, and Whorf,
were they working today, would be considered discourse
analysis. The term was not needed in their time because
then linguistics did not exclude any of the kinds of linguistics they did. (1989: 6)

It is important to realize that the term "discourse analysis" has
been negatively defined (i.e., types of analysis of types of language
that do not fit into the established subfields of linguistics), and that
the types of analysis grouped under this term were not originally
organized under a single category. Although discourse analysis now
enjoys the status of an established subfield of linguistics, it remains a
large and rather open category. The fact that the discourse analyst is
not doing a type of analysis of a type of language that fits into an
older subfield of linguistics, does not mean that she is responsible for
doing *all* of the types of analysis that are left over. Even though a
given study may employ analytical approaches from various disciplines (e.g., linguistics, philosophy, psychology, and sociology), the
types of analysis employed in a given study must be limited by the
analyst, and they are determined, at least in part, by the nature of
the data.

In contrast to analysts whose work fits into one of the previously
established subfields of linguistics referred to above, discourse analysts tend to focus on the fact that language is designed for communication and varies according to contexts of use (see Schiffrin 1987: 3).
Attempting to account for an aspect of language that varies with contexts of use necessarily involves a theoretical bias that incorporates a
socio-cultural perspective. Such a perspective focuses on what
Halliday (1970) describes as the interpersonal function of language,
emphasizing the fact that there is a great deal in language that can
be explained only in terms of a speaker-hearer, interactive context.
This perspective does not exclude what Halliday called the
"ideational function"—the speaker-based, representational, nonin-
teractive aspect of language. However, given the long-standing preference in linguistic analysis for abstracting the "relevant data" away
from interactive contexts of use, thereby highlighting the ideational,
I wish to emphasize that in this work I take a wider perspective on
what counts as "relevant data."

Many researchers who see language as a socio-cultural construct
consider the interpersonal function of language to be crucial to linguis-

tic analysis, and they take interpersonal interaction as the source of many of the characteristic features of language. In the words of Clark and Wilkes-Gibbs:

> Conversation is the fundamental site of language use. For many people, even for whole societies, it is the only site, and it is the primary one for children acquiring language. From this perspective other areas of language use—novels, newspapers, lectures, street signs, rituals—are derivative or secondary. (1986: 3)

Unlike those who would limit the study of language to the identification of abstract competence, many writers draw attention to the fact that there is much in language that can be accounted for only in terms of a speaker-hearer situation of utterance, in which the interpersonal function involving two or more participants has to be considered. Lyons expresses such a view and emphasizes the importance of what he calls the "canonical situation of utterance":

> this involves one-one, or one-many, signalling in the phonic medium along the vocal-auditory channel, with all the participants present in the same actual situation able to see one another and to perceive the associated non-vocal paralinguistic features of their utterances, and each assuming the role of sender and receiver.[6] (1977: 637)

This perspective is also found in the work of Krauss, who writes:

> the addressee is a full participant in the formulation of the message—that is, the vehicle by which meaning is conveyed—and, indeed, may be regarded in a very real sense as the cause of the message. Without the addressee that particular message would not exist. But the message, in the concrete and particular form it takes, is as much attributable to the existence of the addressee as it is to the existence of the speaker. (1987: 96)

In experimental research, Krauss and Glucksberg (1977: 100–103) have demonstrated that children must learn the use of social speech (in addition to linguistic forms) in order to communicate effectively. The authors draw a distinction between social and nonsocial speech, noting that the formulation of nonsocial speech, which is not directed toward another person, does not require consideration of the knowledge and perspective of a particular recipient. By contrast, social messages, which must take into account both the nature of the audience and the context of the conversation, are characterized by variability.

Given the existence of a long tradition of formal linguistic accounts of the way language is, those who see language as a socio-cultural construct have been attempting to state clearly some of the evidence for a view that seeks to encompass *why* language is the way it is. The goal is to identify and describe aspects of human language which depend crucially on viewing language as a social construct (i.e., within interaction) rather than as a biological or psychological construct (i.e., within isolated individuals). An analysis of language that attempts to encompass *why* language is the way it is opens up the field of analysis to consideration of a wide range of factors, including, to name just a few: the speaker's attitude toward the hearer, the speaker's intention, the speaker's assessment of the hearer's knowledge and responses, and concern for "face." Although the inclusion of such variables may complicate the analytic process and make a strictly empirical investigation more difficult, it is the belief of many who endorse a socio-cultural perspective on language use that these factors must be considered if we are to approach an accurate account of the nature of language.

Database

This study is based primarily on the analysis of original data from recorded telephone conversations, and of face-to-face interactions among familiars (primarily in dyads). The participants include eighteen individuals (eleven females and seven males), whose ages ranged from twenty-three to sixty-four (including five in their twenties, five in their thirties, four in their forties, two in their fifties, and two in their sixties).[7] The primary data base, consisting of ten hours of conversation, was collected with two Panasonic Mini-Cassette Recorders (RQ-L317), two Radio Shack Ultra-Miniature Tie Clip Microphones (33-3003), and one Radio Shack Telephone Pickup Device (44-533). The portions of the recordings that contain general extenders were transcribed to include relevant co-text in the form of preceding and subsequent utterances, as well as sufficient detail for a fine-grained analysis. It is worth noting that every instance that occurred in the ten hours of conversation was transcribed. As a result, this corpus can be used to make observations of a quantitative nature (although such observations will be restricted primarily to one section in chapter 2).

I made a conscious decision to collect my own recorded data from spoken interactions among people I knew well, in contexts I was intimately familiar with. I had looked at existing corpora (e.g., Svartvik and Quirk 1980) and was immediately struck by my inability to get "inside" the data or to have any insights into what the transcribed words meant for the individuals who produced them, or how they related to their social contexts of occurrence. I recognize the value of large-scale corpora for the study of the range and frequency of linguistic forms and have benefited from reading previous work involving such corpora (Aijmer 1985, Channell 1994, DuBois 1993); however, existing large-scale corpora seem to exclude some of the most crucial information valued by those undertaking discourse analysis from the perspective of interactional sociolinguistics.

It should be emphasized that the analysis presented in the following pages was based primarily on a study of my own corpus. In analyzing this database, I believe I benefited immeasurably from knowing the participants, their relationships, and their histories, as well as the contexts of their interactions. Throughout this work, in addition to examples from my primary database, I will also cite more than one hundred examples from other sources to illustrate relevant points, and to show that certain phenomena are not restricted to my data set. Some of these examples are from recorded and transcribed conversations (e.g., from other published works). Some examples are from other sources, such as newspapers, magazine articles, advertisements, television shows, and cartoons. Examples from newspapers and magazine articles consist primarily of direct quoted speech from interviews.

Overview

The core of my analysis is presented in chapters 2 through 9. The questions and issues that are addressed in these chapters can be roughly divided into two major groups. I use Halliday's (1970) distinction between the ideational and interpersonal functions of language in order to provide general labels for these two areas.

In chapters 2 through 4, I explore questions related to the ideational, or speaker-based, representational function of language. In chapter 2, I consider the widespead opinion that general extenders are simply examples of vague language, and I explore their potential role as list completers. Specifically, I consider the notion that speakers employ general extenders to indicate that a list is "relevantly incomplete." In addition, I examine the claim that general extenders typically occupy the third "slot" of a list, and that they are employed by English-speakers to satisfy a normative requirement that lists should consist of three parts.

In chapters 3 and 4, I investigate the proposal that speakers use general extenders to implicate a category, so that hearers can infer additional or alternate instances of the category the speaker has in mind. In chapter 3, I explore this potential role of general extenders from the standpoint of the speaker; I look for explicit evidence that speakers treat general extenders as implicating categories, and identify what types of categories seem to be implicated by these expressions. In chapter 4, I consider this proposal from the standpoint of the hearer; I look at what factors help to constrain the interpretation of general extenders, and I discuss whether it is feasible to assume that hearers are able to infer the same category the speaker has in mind.

In chapters 5 through 9, I argue that when viewed within their role in the interactive exchange of talk, general extenders appear to have a function that is interpersonal and tied to the social relationships of the participants. The analysis in chapter 5 builds on the preceding discussion of category implication and discusses how interlocutors manage to create a compatibility of categories, despite the fact that individual mental worlds are necessarily distinct. A crucial concept explored in this discussion is the nature of intersubjectivity. I argue that general extenders serve to mark an assumption of shared knowledge and experience, which may help to establish and maintain a sense of rapport among the interlocutors.

In chapter 6, I explore the role of expectations in speakers' use of general extenders. I also demonstrate how speakers may employ certain expressions (e.g., *or anything, or something, and everything, and all (that)*) as intensifiers, to emphasize a preceding part of an utterance and to mark an attitude toward a message expressed. We will see how speakers, in using general extenders as intensifiers, may express an evaluation of something as surprising or extreme, or draw attention to and clarify intentions.

In chapter 7, I consider how a speaker's use of a general extender may be viewed as a politeness strategy. I illustrate how adjunctive general extenders (in particular the form *and stuff*) may function as markers of invited solidarity (a strategy of positive politeness), and how disjunctive general extenders (i.e., *or something, or anything, or whatever*) may function as markers of possible alternatives (a strategy of negative politeness).

In chapters 8 and 9, I consider general extenders from the perspective of expectations associated with cooperative interaction, such as those proposed by Grice (1975). In chapter 8, I consider how *disjunctive* general extenders may be viewed as hedges on the maxim of Quality "Be truthful"). In chapter 9, I show how *adjunctive* general extenders may be used to demonstrate an orientation to the maxim of Quantity "Don't say too much or too little").

Finally, in chapter 10, I summarize the findings presented throughout this work, provide a synthesis of the functions associated with the most frequently occurring forms, and attempt to illustrate the multifunctionality of these widely used forms.

PART TWO

Ideational Function

Vague Language and List Construction

Jerry: Well let me ask you this, what exactly did you say
         when you asked her out?
George: I said "Would you like to go for a walk or
         something."
Jerry: O::h, a wa::lk, we:ll
George: O:r something, I said "O:R SOMETHING."
Jerry: Or something. (2.0) Yeah, that's a date.
George: There you go.

                              Seinfeld episode 1995

The transcribed extract above is from an episode of the American
television program *Seinfeld*. It is one of the few instances I have observed in which a general extender and its meaning are actually discussed by those who use it. Notice that, for the speakers, there is a
significant difference between the expressions *go for a walk* and *go for
a walk or something*. These speakers actually conclude that the
general extender has a major impact on what is communicated.

Vague Language

In spite of this type of evidence, there seems to be a much more
widespread opinion that general extenders make no contribution to
communication. They are treated as examples of "vague language"
which has low or negative value. In one reported study, Dines (1980)
found that middle-class judges in Australia associated the use of
general extenders with working-class speech. They also indicated

that the forms were stigmatized because they were "assumed to reflect vague and inexplicit speech" (1980: 19). It is this association with vagueness that results in the inclusion of general extenders in one chapter of Channell's book *Vague Language* (1994). Channell cites, without a reference, a suggestion that these forms are "purely performance 'fillers,' introduced to give both speaker, and hearer, additional time for processing" (1994: 120). In her analysis, Channell does not pursue this issue, focusing instead on category implication.

The negative value attached to the use of general extenders seems to come from a feeling that vagueness in reference indicates vagueness in thinking, and hence stupidity. In the following example, Homer Simpson (a father figure from the American television show and comic strip *The Simpsons*) characterizes the way young, uneducated people talk "these days" by imitating how he thinks they speak (*Simpsons Comics* 1994: 2).

[1]   Homer: It's, like, they're all stupid **and stuff.**

The general extender *and stuff* is treated in this case as an indicator of the speech style of the young and poorly educated. Excerpt [2], from a cartoon in a daily newspaper, presents a similar characterization of the type of person who uses such "vague" language. The cartoon depicts a teenager in baggy clothes, leaning against a lamppost and listening to a Walkman. The headline of a newspaper lying at his feet is: *Cities fight truancy.* The caption above his head says:

[2]   I usually, like, spend my day hangin' out on the street,
      listenin' to tunes, bummin' with friends **and stuff** . . . but
      when the school-year ends, I try to relax more!
      (*Honolulu Advertiser*, 14 July 1996)

In addition to being young and poorly educated, this teenager is portrayed as sloppy and lazy—and likely to say *and stuff.* The prevalence—even among some linguists—of the opinion that vagueness in reference is an indication of vagueness in thinking has been a constant surprise to me while I have been studying these forms. Although it may have a limited impact, I hope that the analysis presented in the following chapters will dispel the notion that general extenders are simply empty fillers, or vague, meaningless forms.

There have been several attempts to identify a more useful role for general extenders. In this chapter, I review one proposal that general extenders have an identifiable role in the construction of lists, and that they are specifically used to complete three-part lists.

List Construction

Jefferson has claimed that, in constructing lists, speakers and hearers in natural conversation orient to what she calls the "programmatic relevance of three partedness" (1990: 66). In other words, participants are aware of the fact that "lists not only can and do occur in three parts, but *should* so occur" (1990: 66). Working in the tradition of conversation analysis, Jefferson proposes that general extenders (which she calls "generalized list completers") are employed by conversational participants to complete three-part lists, and that these expressions provide a "methodic solution to the problem of three-partedness" (1990: 67).

Examples [3]–[5], from my corpus, would seem to support the claim that general extenders function to complete three-part lists. In each instance, a speaker names two items and finishes the list with a general extender.

[3]   (Julie and Rosie are planning a camping trip)
   1. Julie: John and I are hiking out with you.
   2. Rosie: Ya:::y
   3. Julie: He's excited about the idea. We went an' bought shoes.
   4. Rosie: Okay. That's //cool.
   5. Julie: So—
   6. Rosie: We'll get an early start, an' I was thinking if we wanted to bring in the coo::ler, we could, an' have it—each pitch in a little bit of money an' have Mike take it out by boat. So that we can put all the kitchen stuff in the::re, an' all the heavy stuff, an' just pack out our clo::thes an' tents **an' stuff**.

[4]   (Sara and Roger are discussing her plans to move to a town that Roger and his wife are familiar with)
   1. Sara: the first (.) order of importance is to find a place to li::ve.
   2. Roger: Right. (.) Ah, yeah. We've made a list of you— for you of like doctors a::nd connections, **an' thi//ngs**
   3. Sara: Yea:::h.
   4. Roger: Yea::h You'll find a place to live, and you'll find a job. Don't worry about that.
   5. Sara: Oh, no. I'm not worried about that at all.

[5]   (Blake and Donna are in the kitchen preparing their dinner)
   1. Donna: There's garlic salt an' onion powder **an' things like (that)**—

2. Blake: Okay.
3. Donna: An'
4. Blake: Ble:::ck! There's lima beans in he:::re!
5. Donna: I'll eat 'em.

In addition to suggesting that general extenders are used to complete three-part lists, Jefferson notes that these expressions are typically used where lists are "relevantly incomplete" (1990: 68). That is, even if a third item were named, the list would not be exhaustively given. (An exception to this occurs when the speaker uses the general extender to fill the third slot, and also to hold the floor temporarily while she searches for the third item in a list of three. This will be illustrated with excerpt [6].) On the other hand, a list consisting of three explicitly named items is "relatively complete"; the named items "exhaust the possible array of nameables for the purposes to which this particular listing is being put" (Jefferson, 1990: 68).

It is not hard to imagine more than one item that could be added to each of the lists which appear in the above exchanges. For instance, in [3], additional light items that Rosie and Julie might take camping include sleeping bags, sheets, and towels. The possible "things" to which Roger refers in [4] might be references of other service providers that Sara would find useful in a new town, such as hairdressers, dentists, and car mechanics. Finally, in [5], Donna directs Blake to the cabinet containing spices and herbs for cooking, where one might also expect to find basil, rosemary, thyme, parsley, and oregano.

Another example that appears to demonstrate a speaker's orientation to the three-part nature of lists is found in [6]. Here Roger mentions two things, and after an unsuccessful search for a third, he fills the slot with a general extender.

[6]   (Sara and Roger are discussing the possibility that his landlord will let her take over his apartment when he leaves)

1. Sara: So what's the story on that apartment, has anybody come by an' looked at it?
2. Roger: No, we've had a call from the u::m (.) like the agent saying somebody is planning to come, a::n' would that—would it be okay if they call us, an' an' an' **and so on**=the person come an' look at it // (it's **)
3. Sara: I can't beli//eve that, man. When you've got somebody li:ned up who's willin' to like plunk down their money an' they don't like—Wull, nevermind.
4. Roger: Yeah.

In [6], Roger's account of what the agent said may be seen to consist of three parts: (1) *somebody is planning to come*; (2) *and would it be okay if they call us*; (3) and *and so on*. As it turns out, the general extender *and so on* is subsequently specified by the following phrase *the person come and look at it*. This example seems to support an argument that the general extender is used to fill the third slot where the speaker is, at least temporarily, unable to produce a third item. In this case, Roger's replacement of the general extender *and so on* with the third item *the person come by an' look at it* would indicate that the list is then "relatively complete."

The Problem of Three-Partedness

Although examples [3]–[6] may be viewed as support for the claim that general extenders can be used to complete three-part lists, they do not provide sufficient evidence to support the larger claim that participants employ these expressions to solve a "problem of three-partedness." In order to consider this possibility, we must take a closer look at the nature of Jefferson's claim.

Based on the emphasized use of the word *should*, it appears that Jefferson's (1990: 66–67) intention is to treat participants' orientation to three-partedness as a *norm*. Indeed, as Bilmes (1986: 175) notes, "norms are often defined in terms of an 'ought.'" Broadly speaking, a norm can be defined as follows:

> A norm is a rule of a certain type. A rule may prescribe the actions that constitute a certain activity (e.g., the rules of chess . . .). A norm, on the other hand, regulates activities. It specifies when the activity should, may, or should not be done, or how the activity can be carried out in a socially acceptable manner. A norm is thus a regulative rule. Once again, though, a norm is only a regulative rule of a certain type. . . . A norm is enforced and remedied by community members in their relations with one another. Regulations are enforced from without. (Bilmes 1986: 171)

Researchers have proposed various criteria for identifying norms. One method relies on statistical distributions of behavior (Bilmes 1986: 172). If something is a norm, it will be a frequent occurrence.

A quantitative analysis of 156 occurrences of general extenders from recorded telephone conversations and face-to-face interactions (i.e., all of the instances of general extenders in my data set) reveals that general extenders are used to complete three-part lists in approximately 32 instances (the need to approximate the number of instances will be discussed below). Among the 124 remaining instances, there are eight list-like constructions that appear to exceed three parts. These may be seen to exhibit the structure [3 items + general extender], where the general extender fills the fourth "slot." Examples include the following:

[7]   (Jean is speaking with her daughter, Julie)
    1. Julie: You takin' a nap?
    2. Jean: No:::=I've been (.) vacuumin' 'n (1.0) washin':
       (1.0) clo::thes 'n dustin': **'n: all that stuff.**
    3. Julie: Umhm.

[8] 1. Maya: You know that girl? I don't know her name.
       I can't remember her name I don't know why. The girl
       that has braids in her hair all the ti:me that used to
       sing for Andy's band, and an' Margaret has the hots fo:r
       an' a//ll that stuff?
    2. Sara: O:h yeah. We—her Wendy=
    3. Maya: =Wendy. That's right.

There are no clear examples in my corpus of lists of the form [4(+) items + general extender]. However, this does not mean that such structures never occur. We will look at one example, excerpt [2] in chapter 4, that contains five items before the general extender.

By far the most common structure identified in the data, occurring approximately 116 times, is of the form [1 item + general extender]. Excerpts [9]–[11] are offered as examples.

[9] 1. William: Are any of the uh trees turning?
    2. Julie: U:m they don't really turn much here I don't
       think.
    3. William: They don't
    4. Julie: Yeah.
    5. William: Yeah. Most of 'em are evergreens around
       there I guess. Pine trees **an' stuff.**

[10]   (Maya is describing a *Creep Show* movie)
    1. Maya: I like the one where they have the—the
       animal locked in a bo:x and the—the woman (.5)
       what's her name—his wife is real bitchy an' he was
       having fantasies of ways to kill her? He was like a
       scie//ntist **or something?**
    2. Sara: That was in the first o:ne I didn't see it.

[11]   (Sara is talking about her sister's bouts with depression)
    1. Sara: I know when my sister is depressed I can't (.)
       imagine—I mean I think I get miserable an' (.) like my
       mom told me though—w—They talked with the

psychiatrist **an' all**— but she said y—uh know as
depressed as you ever get, you know she's three times
that depressed an' can't get out of it.= An' doesn't know
that there's any end to it. You know when I'm at the
bottom of the pi://le I'm like
2. Maya: Right.

Since general extenders occur as third parts in only 32 of 156 instances,
we might argue that the remaining 124 examples provide counterevi-
dence to Jefferson's (1990) claim that participants employ these
expressions to solve a "problem of three-partedness" (1990: 67). However, there is a further point to consider: How do we know whether
all of these examples constitute lists?

The Nature of Lists

Jefferson does not explore how one might distinguish a list from a non-
list, nor does she discuss the origin of the assumed "programmatic
relevance of three partedness" (1990: 66).[1] It is possible, however,
that her analysis of list construction was inspired by an observation
made by Sacks (1972), which was subsequently explored in a study by
Bilmes (1982): that two instances are needed to establish a pattern
and an expectation, and that a third instance is required to confirm
the pattern and the expectation. If, in "doing listing" with general
extenders as third parts, we are essentially establishing a pattern
and an expectation with two items, and confirming it via the general
extender, then structures of the form [1 item + general extender] might
be viewed as lacking the required number of items to establish a pattern and expectation.

How many items are required to indicate that one is "doing
listing"? At least one researcher (Lerner 1994: 23–24) has suggested
that three parts are required. If this is so, then an example of the
structure [1 item + general extender] might be interpreted as something other than a list. (Such examples will receive further attention
in chapters 6 through 9.) Note that if we remove the 116 examples of
the structure [1 item + general extender] from the total number of
examples (156), we are left with only 40 examples that consist of at
least three parts. Since general extenders occur as third parts in 32 of
these 40 examples (or 80 percent), we might indeed argue that, where
general extenders occur in lists, they typically occur as the third item.

What about examples of the structure [3(+) items + general
extender]? Would examples consisting of more than three parts be
considered lists? It seems so. The following excerpt is taken from
Schiffrin's article "Making a List."

[12] Like he has candy
      and ice cream,
      and uh a little milk maybe
      and bread,
      stuff like that.
      (1994b: 401)

In this example, the speaker names four items that can be bought at a small store and then concludes the list with a general extender.

Assuming that lists have a minimum of three parts, structures of the form [3(+) items + general extender] might be considered superfluous, in that they provide more instances than are required. However, a consideration of the speaker's purpose in producing a list may lead to an alternative analysis. For example, returning to example [7], it may be that Jean's goal is to emphasize how much work she has been doing, rather than to establish a pattern or expectation. On being asked *You takin' a nap?*, Jean responds *No:::=I've been (.) vacuumin' 'n (1.0) washin': (1.0) clo::thes 'n dustin': 'n: all that stuff.* It is important to consider carefully what Jean is saying, because in responding to Julie's question in this manner, Jean has chosen a longer response rather than simply naming the activity "housework." Jean's response might be seen to exhibit iconicity between message content ("I have been doing a lot of work") and form (naming several instances of an activity and creating a longer message, rather than simply naming the whole activity, "housework"). The length of this particular message is also increased by extended pauses and lengthened vowels. Indeed, recent research has suggested, in Kirsner's words, that:

> language is less arbitrary and less purely symbolic than has previously been assumed and that there is an appreciable iconic relationship between the physical form of grammatical structures and the content of messages which these structures are used to communicate. (1985: 249)

Haiman (1980, 1983) has also described this type of iconicity in some detail. Viewed from this alternative perspective, Jean's set of household chores can still be interpreted as "doing listing" with a general extender, but not for the purpose of establishing a pattern in order to confirm it.

Problems with the List-style Analysis

An attempt to implement a list-style analysis reveals problems of applicability. Note that excerpts [3]–[5] contain simple examples of three-part lists consisting of distinct entities. However, in those instances where the "parts" being described are other than distinct entities, it is sometimes quite difficult to identify each of those parts.[2] With contextualized examples such as those offered below in [13] and [14], we can begin to understand the nature of this analytic problem. For example, in excerpt [13] there are several connected propositions that may be treated as a list of things known about Frederico. Alternatively, some of the propositions may be treated as reasons for stating other propositions on the same list. Or there may be more than one list being articulated—depending, for example, on whether we view coming "from a really wealthy family" as an attribute of Frederico or as a cause of his having "had a lot of experiences." In short, identifying items in a potential list becomes more difficult when we go beyond simple nouns (I will return to this issue in chapter 4).

[13]   (Crystal is telling Julie about some guys she just met)
  1. Crystal: Yeah. Um Frederico is just super—he's super mature for his age though, 'cause he's he sailed around the world s—um (.) for four yea::rs and (.) just sorta— an' had older brothers y'kno::w, and come from a really wealthy family::=had a lot of experiences **and stuff,** so he really (1.0) kinda presents himself as being older.
  2. Julie: Umhm. . .

[14]   (Sara is outlining what her plans will be after moving to the city where Roger resides)
  1. Sara: . . .because really what I'm planning on doing is when I get out there .hhh I'm first going to focus my energy on like finding a place to li:::ve =
  2. Roger: =Right=
  3. Sara: =for the first couple of da::ys
  4. Roger: Ri//ght
  5. Sara: an' the::n I'm gonna go do::wn (.) or I might go down to a temporary place an' like do a little testing .hhh a//n'
  6. Roger: Right.
  7. Sara: start sendin' out my resumé, **an' stuff like that,** but, I me//an,
  8. Roger: Right.
  9. Sara: the first (.) order of importance is to find a place to li::ve.
  10. Roger: Right. . . .

In instances such as [13] and [14], the identification of parts will necessarily be a subjective determination made by the analyst, as would the decision that the speaker is necessarily constructing a list.

A second and more significant problem with the list-style analysis is that it is exclusively structural; it fails to consider why interactional participants would orient to a norm of three-partedness. Assuming that a speaker is establishing a pattern and an expectation in forming a list, an obvious question is: What kind of pattern and expectation? Moreover, we might intuitively recognize the role of some general extenders in lists, but remain cautious about defining them (e.g., as "list completers") by their occasional occurrence in that role.

Rather than dwell on the shortcomings of this analysis, I will move on in the next chapter to consider the much more powerful claim that general extenders function as category-implicative expressions.

–3–

Category Implication

In the accompanying cartoon (figure 3.1), Curtis is with his family in his mother's hospital room. When his mother gains consciousness, his father asks him to take his younger brother home. Puzzled by the father's request, as they are leaving the hospital, the younger brother asks Curtis "Why did we have to leave?" In response to his brother's question, Curtis provides an answer containing a general extender: *They wanna kiss and hug and stuff like that.* It is possible that Curtis is just constructing a list of behaviors. Intuitively, however, we might suspect that Curtis isn't communicating a list of behaviors, but is characterizing a kind of behavior. The kind, or category of behavior he may have in mind is exemplified by the actions described, but not named as a general category. In his brother's subsequent response, those actions are given a general category label, (i.e., *mushy stuff*). The joke, of course, is that the child's general category descriptor (*mushy*) is so predictably at odds with the suggested grown-up's general category descriptor (*romantic*) for the set of actions. In order to understand why this cartoon is humorous, we have

Figure 3.1. Curtis. (Copyright 1995 by King Features Syndicate. Reprinted with special permission of King Features Syndicate.)

to recognize how the same set of behaviors can be interpreted in terms of two quite distinct categories.

This example of a general extender being used in a (somewhat stylized) context serves to introduce a quite different approach to the analysis of these forms. This approach depends on assigning human experiences to categories, analyzing how these categories are expressed, and discovering how we, as analysts, can determine what kinds of categories speakers may have in mind, as evidenced by what they say. As part of that evidence, general extenders have been treated by a number of researchers as examples of the categorization process at work (Aijmer 1985, Ball and Ariel 1978, Channell 1994, Dines 1980, Ward and Birner 1993). In essence, general extenders have been analyzed as if their primary function were category implication. In pursuing this type of analysis, researchers have separated general extenders from their actual contexts of use, largely disregarding sociolinguistic factors; they have taken a mainly psycholinguistic perspective, focusing on the possible role of general extenders as clues to cognitive processing. By taking this narrow perspective, analysts have been able to gain some insights both into the nature of categorization and into one possible function of general extenders.

The categorization perspective can be summarized in the following way: In using a general extender, (e.g., *and stuff like that*), in combination with a named exemplar (e.g., *kiss and hug*), a speaker implicates a category so that a hearer can infer additional or alternate members of a category that the speaker has in mind. This perspective is more precisely described by Aijmer, who suggests that if a general extender begins with the conjunction *and*, the "speaker instructs the listener to pick out all the members of the set on the basis of the member (or members) which has been produced as an example," and that if a general extender begins with or, "the speaker signals to the listener to pick out one (some) member of the same set as the preceding member" (1985: 374). In this chapter, I will explore this potential role of general extenders in cognitive processing, essentially looking at the subject from the standpoint of the speaker. Questions to be addressed in this chapter include: What explicit evidence is there to suggest that speakers treat general extenders as category implicative expressions? Why would a speaker use a general extender to implicate a category, when the category can be more directly referred to by name? Before I address these questions, however, it is necessary to take a closer look at the nature of categorization.[1]

Categorization

Categorization plays a crucial role in human cognition, yet we give little thought to this process. Indeed, it seems that most of us have a very simple idea of how categorization works: we take for granted that categories have clear boundaries, and that all members of a given category must have something in common. If we consider the purpose of categorization, we see that it is not surprising that we hold such a view.

Why do we categorize? Categorization is the means by which we identify objects in the world and reduce the perceived complexity of our environment; it is the means by which we divide the world into manageable chunks (see Bruner et al. 1956: 12). In order to interpret the vast continuum of the world around us, we simplify it: we treat it as consisting of meaningful groupings. Interestingly, we tend to lose track of the fact that we impose divisions on the world around us; and we come to assume that our human categories correlate with the Real World. In fact, a close examination of human categories reveals that they do not fit the world as it really is. As we consider the possible role of general extenders as category implicative expressions, this is a crucial point to keep in mind.

Overview of Theories

Within the past fifty years or so, theories of categorization have changed dramatically. The consensus among scholars has gone from a classical view of categories as well-defined, context-independent, and pre-stored in memory, to a contemporary view of categories as fuzzy-edged, context-dependent, and computable within a given situation. Perceptual similarity was once assumed to be the primary basis of categorization, but it is now considered insufficient. Factors such as background knowledge, memory, and imagination are recognized as some of the complex sources that determine how categories are formed. In the following sections I present a brief overview of how this radical change of perspective has come about.

The Classical View

Until the latter part of the twentieth century, the assumption that human categories correlated with the Real World was widely accepted among scholars. This perspective on categorization has been called the "classical view." According to the classical view, categories are considered to be:

> discrete, absolute and pristine, be they God-given, as Plato
> or Descartes would have it; neuro-genetically "wired-in"
> as Chomsky (1966, 1968) or Bickerton (1981) would have it;

representing stable features of The Real World as Russell (1905, 1919), Carnap (1947, 1959) and other positivists would have it; or made out of atomic units of perception as the classical empiricists would have it. (Givón 1984: 12–13)

Category membership is determined by necessary and sufficient conditions, or by the possession of criterial properties. In other words, all members of a category must have certain features in common. This is illustrated in figure 3.2, where *a* represents a criterial property, *b* is a member possessing that property, and *c* is a nonmember, which does not possess it. Note that key components of this perspective include the ideas that categories are well-defined, context-independent, stable, and based on perception.

The Contemporary View

Over the past few decades, categorization has been the focus of a substantial amount of scholarship in many different areas. The phenomenon has been studied by philosophers (e.g., Allwood et al. 1977, Wittgenstein 1953, Zadeh 1965), anthropologists (e.g., Bateson 1955, Berlin 1978, Berlin et al. 1968, Bilmes 1988, Dougherty 1981, Frake 1969, Lounsbury 1964), psychologists (e.g., Barsalou 1983, 1987; Bruner et al. 1956; Miller 1978; Neisser 1987; Nelson 1983; Rosch 1977, 1978; Vygotsky 1962), linguists (e.g., Cruse 1986; Givón 1984; Grace 1987; Jackendoff 1985; Labov 1973; G. Lakoff 1972, 1987a, 1987b; Taylor 1995; Tsohatzidis 1990), and sociologists (e.g., Cicourel 1974, Sacks 1992). While scholars from these diverse areas have not resolved all of their differences on this issue, something close to a consensus can be identified (Neisser 1987: vii), in terms of a commit-

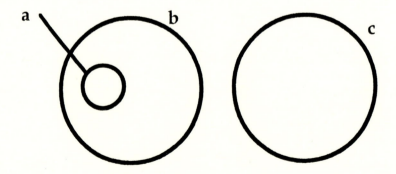

Figure 3.2. The classical view.

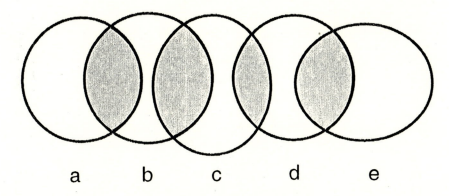

Figure 3.3. The Wittgenstein view.

ment to what I am generally characterizing as the "contemporary view."

The contemporary view of categorization refutes nearly every aspect of the classical view. Among the first scholars to challenge the classical view was Wittgenstein (1953), who proposed that concepts (or categories) are fuzzy-edged, or "uncircumscribed" (1953, vol. 1: 70). Wittgenstein argued that, rather than finding a property common to all members of a category by virtue of which we group them together, an examination of our concepts reveals "a complicated network of similarities overlapping and criss-crossing: sometimes overall similarities, sometimes similarities of detail" (1953, vol. 1: 66). The relationship between members of a category, as described by Wittgenstein, is represented by figure 3.3. In this view, a member *a* may share properties with *b*, *b* may share properties with *c, c* may share properties with *d*, and *d* may share properties with *e*; however, it may be the case that *a* and *e* do not share any common properties. This type of relationship was described by Wittgenstein in terms of "family resemblances" (1953, vol. 1: 67).

The contemporary notion of category has also been greatly influenced by the work of Rosch (1974, 1977, 1978). Like Wittgenstein, Rosch proposed that "most, if not all categories do not have clear-cut boundaries" (1978: 35), and that the classification of an object is not simply determined by a certain set of defining features. Rather, there is no single feature that every member of a category must possess. Through a series of experiments, Rosch and a number of others (see Rosch and Mervis 1975, Rosch et al. 1976, Mervis and Rosch 1981, Medin and Smith 1984, Oden 1987, Smith and Medin 1981) showed that categories have a graded structure: at the center of each category is a prototype, which exhibits the highest concentration of characteristic properties; and toward the undefined edges of the category, members exhibit the fewest characteristic properties and may barely count as members. This prototype view of categorization can be represented by the following illustration. In figure 3.4, the letters *a, b, c,* and *d* represent characteristic properties; a member possessing all four would be found in the shaded area and would be a prototype. For example, Rosch's studies demonstrated that the prototypical or "best" example of a chair is the four-legged, straight-backed variety often found in dining rooms. Modern, single-pedestal chairs are less typical, and certain varieties, such as the large beanbag on the floor, hardly count as chairs at all. This so-called graded structure is now widely believed to characterize most, if not all, categories (see Neisser 1987: 3).[2] Support for the existence of "graded structure" is also to be found in the results of a test in which participants were presented with pictures of containers and asked to label them *cup, vase,* or *bowl*. Using this test, Labov (1973) demonstrated that the boundaries between these words were not as precisely defined as they would have to be if they denoted categories determined by necessary and sufficient conditions. In other words, it is easier to choose what a really clear (or prototypical) example of the category *cup* is, than to decide where the boundary of that category must lie.

It follows that, if categories have neither clear boundaries nor necessary and sufficient conditions, it would be impossible to capture the entire class of items (i.e., the members) that would potentially be

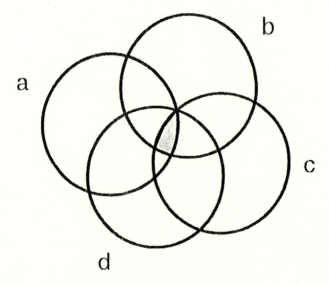

Figure 3.4. The prototype view.

found in a given category. The inability to provide a semantic, or decompositional, account of the members' properties does not mean, however, that there are no restrictions on the items that might be included in a given category (see G. Lakoff 1987a). Among the factors that help to constrain the interpretation of what may be included in a category are context (linguistic and nonlinguistic), background knowledge, and experience (this point will be discussed in chapter 4).

Recent Developments in the Contemporary View

Within the past decade or so, research has further challenged the classical view, with evidence that category structure is not stable but dynamic, and that it may vary across individuals and time (Barsalou 1987, G. Lakoff 1987b, Neisser 1987, Shimron and Chernitsky 1995). In simple terms, while grandfather's *radio* (that large wooden cabinet) might have been considered within the category of *furniture*, his granddaughter's *radio* (a Walkman) probably is not (Overstreet and Yule 1997a).

Recent investigations have also determined that the notion of similarity is insufficient to account for the structure of categories. This is because similarity is a subjective judgment and depends on the weight assigned to a particular feature. For example, given a *banana*, an *orange*, and a *ball*, you might initially think that the *banana* and the *orange* are more similar. However, the *orange* and the *ball* might be judged to be more similar if the feature "round" were given sufficient weight. As a result of this observation, we now view categories as having a much more complex source. In fact, the process of categorization is currently treated much more like problem-solving than attribute-matching. To illustrate this point, Murphy and Medin (1985: 295) note that while "jumping into a swimming pool with one's clothes on" is not directly associated with the concept "intoxicated," observation of this behavior in a particular situation might be used to classify a person as "drunk"; however, in a context where someone is in danger of drowning, the same behavior may lead to the classification of the person as a "hero." An individual's ability to perform such categorization is based on a number of factors, including memory, imagination, and background knowledge. For more on the complex sources of categorization, see Gelman et al. (1994), Keil (1991), G. Lakoff (1987a), and Medin (1989).

The topic of categorization is a complex one, and I have presented only a rough outline here. At present, a matter of some debate in the study of categorization is the question whether categorization is purely intellectual and based on mental models or beliefs about the world, or whether it also has a perceptual or ecological basis.[3] It is possible that this issue may never really be resolved, because, as Neisser (1987: 5) notes, "a complete understanding of categories and concepts may be impossible without an equally complete understanding of the world itself."

General Extenders as Category Implicative Expressions

Most of the preceding discussion has focused on the fact that categorization plays a crucial role in human cognition, but we should also recognize that categorization plays an important role in communication, where it allows for economy of expression. Rather than naming individual members of a category, a speaker can refer to them collectively. If a collective name for the category does not come to mind immediately, the speaker can employ some linguistic means to imply the category.

If general extenders are to be analyzed as a linguistic means of implicating a category of some kind, then it would be helpful to find explicit evidence in the data that speakers treat them as such. An examination of my database reveals that speakers using a general extender do not typically go on to make explicit mention of what was implicated by their use of that general extender. There are, however, some perspicuous cases, in which speakers subsequently specify some of the additional or alternate things that seem to have been implied by their use of a general extender. Excerpts [1]–[5] contain examples of such cases.

In [1], Sara is describing her cat's behavior on a recent visit to the vet.

[1] 1. Sara: Y'know an' like uh (his emotional—) He was so
              good when I took him back to the vet to have him
              looked at?
     2. Roger: Oh, he didn't have to be sedated?
     3. Sara: No::, like, w—I mean, they just went an' sh—
              looked at him, she took his temperature, an' y'know
              stuck the thermometer up his butt, an' he didn't howl **or
              anything**. He didn't fi:::ght, or hiss, or scratch, **or
              anything**. He just kinda stoo:d the//re.
     4. Roger: Oh
     5. Sara: I was like 'Cool!' I was so::: pleased.

Sara reports that her cat was well-behaved and says that despite the vet's probing examination, *he didn't howl or anything*. Sara then elaborates on what the *or anything* might have been: *He didn't fight, or hiss, or scratch, or anything. He just kinda stood there.* The category implicated by the first use of *or anything* in [1] might be described as "the ways in which a cat might misbehave at the vet's office." The second use of *or anything* within this elaboration seems to indicate that there are still further alternative ways in which the cat might have protested the examination, or misbehaved.

In [2], Sara and Maya are talking about a mutual friend's (Wendy's) mistreatment of animals, and her recent decision to have her dog put to sleep.

[2] 1. Maya: she's just really weird with them—she
          doesn't—I mean I—I think she's alm//ost like—
     2. Sara: It's like a completely unconscious sadistic
          str//eak.
     3. Maya: Yeah it is. It's very sadistic. It's really mean.
          (.5) The whole thing is r(h)eally m(h)ean when you
          watch her and she's like—gets kind of absorbed with it
          but she's not really.=I don't think she believes that
          they're living at all.
     4. Sara: Um//hm
     5. Maya: I don't think she believes that they'll like (.)
          bleed **an' stuff**. I don't think she understands that (.)
          when she gassed her dog that the dog bloated and lost
          oxygen and choked to death and (.) twitched and then
          died you know.

According to Maya, Wendy doesn't grasp the fact that animals are living creatures that have a capacity for suffering. In turn 5, Maya contends that Wendy doesn't believe *that they'll like bleed an' stuff*. She then expounds upon the expression *an' stuff*: *I don't think she understands that when she gassed her dog that the dog bloated and lost oxygen and choked to death and twitched and then died you know*. It would appear that for Maya, bleeding, bloating, choking, twitching, and dying are members of a category of "ways in which living creatures may suffer."

In excerpt [3], Crystal is telling her friend Julie about some young men from Argentina she has just met.

[3] 1. Julie: Frederico, huh?
     2. Crystal: Frederico=I know! An' his brother is Juan. huh
          huh // huh
     3. Julie: O:::h, look out!
     4. Crystal: Juan is one of those light ones. He has red hair
          an' everything. L—Light hair, blue eyes, (.) white
          skin, Mex—um, uh Spanish, y'know.
     5. Julie: Umhm

6. Crystal: An' Frederico he's—he's d<u>a::</u>rk. He's um—he's
really nice.

In turn 4, Crystal describes Juan as *one of those light ones. He has red hair and everything*. Her further characterization indicates that at least part of *everything* includes: *light hair, blue eyes,* and *white skin*. In this example, *and everything* implicates a category of physical features that "light" Spanish people are presumed to have.

In excerpt [4], Sara and Maya are talking about a gay friend of theirs.

[4] 1. Sara: John's looking for a girlfriend.
   2. Maya: Oh, a cover girlfriend?
   3. Sara: Yeah.
   4. Maya: Co//ol.
   5. Sara: No. W—he's like (.) like "You know," he's like
       "Can you help me out here?" an' I huh I went "John" Ø
       "I'm looking for a girlfriend" an' I was like
   6. Maya: "Why?"
   7. Sara: Hey. Ø "Well just one to hang out with you know
       somebody just to hang out an' do stuff with **an' an'
       everything** you know maybe I dunno, maybe once in a
       while get drunk and make out with—n<u>o</u>t to have se:x, I
       wouldn't want to have s<u>e</u>x, y'know, just y'know, some
       girl to hang out with." I'm like (.) // "I don't know
       man."
   8. Maya: huh "I: can't even do that. Whatta ya—" huh
       huh "Whatta you want from me, bl<u>oo</u>d?" Oh well.
   9. Sara: Heh! He's like "Do you know anybody? who—
       who would be into that?" Ø "No I sure don't. Everybody
       I know wants sex."
  10. Maya: "Everybody I know wants some kind of soft parts
       rubbed up against their soft parts. Or in their facial
       area **or something**."
  11. Sara: Yea//h.
  12. Maya: "Something—something in the p<u>oo</u>ntang arena."

There are two general extenders that are elaborated on in this excerpt: *and everything* in turn 7, and *or something* in turn 10. In turn 7, Sara reports John's description of what he wants a girlfriend for. In Sara's report of John's description, the *and everything* includes hanging out, getting drunk, and making out, but not having sex. In this example, the category of things referred to by the general extender *and everything* might be called "things John wants to do with his girlfriend."

The second example of a perspicuous case in excerpt [4] is found in turns 10 and 12. In turn 10 Maya says: *Everybody I know wants some kind of soft parts rubbed up against their soft parts. Or in their facial area or something.* She then goes on to state explicitly a thing that might have been implicated by the expression *or something*: *Something—something in the poontang arena.* The category referred to by Maya in this particular context might be called "the places that everybody wants some kind of soft parts rubbed up against."

Finally, in excerpt [5], Sara and Maya are discussing old age, and the importance of being satisfied with one's life.

[5] 1. Maya: . . . unfortunately the grandma I like best is not— dudn't feel like you know her life has been (.) any good so:

  2. Sara: Well I—I—I hope that if I get to that age—if I make it to that age and I look back and start (.) thinking that what I've done has not been you know that I will have the ba:lls **or the—the whatever**—the gumption // to=

  3. Maya: hnh!

  4. Sara: =get up and go do something no:w (.) rather than just sit there and go=

  5. Maya: (**)

  6. Sara: ="Oh well. I never did anything. I guess that's okay." I mean (.) you're gonna keel over and die within the next couple of weeks then 'cause you've lost your will.

  7. Maya: Ri:ght.

In turns 2 and 4, Sara subsequently specifes an alternative instance that is implicated by the general extender *or whatever*: *I will have the ba:lls or the—the whatever—the gumption to get up and go do something now . . . .* In this case, the general extender might be seen to implicate a category of "characteristics that will enable Sara to take action."

Note that the perspicuous cases presented above contain various general extenders: [1] *or anything*; [2] *and stuff*; [3] *and everything*; [4] *and everything, or something*; [5] *or whatever.* Indeed, it appears that most general extenders have the capacity to function as category implicative expressions. (More narrowly specified functions of individual forms will be explored in chapters 6–9.)[4]

Having established the potential function of general extenders as a means of implicating categories, we can now look more closely at the nature of categories that typically are implicated in this way.

Lexicalized versus Nonlexicalized Categories

By and large, the discussion of categories, whether in the classical or the contemporary view, has focused on what have been called "natural" or "common" categories, with labels such as *bird, fruit,* or *furniture.* As illustrated by these labels, common categories are lexicalized—that is, they are encoded as single lexical items. The investigation of common categories has typically been undertaken through experimental tests with constructed examples in restricted contexts, as in the category verification task format, in which subjects are asked to decide, for example, whether *bat* and *chair* are members of the category *bird* (see Rosch 1975a, 1975b, Rosch et al. 1976, Rosch and Mervis 1975, Smith et al. 1974). This extremely narrow perspective on the nature of categories and the process of categorization has provided no insights into what people do when a single lexical item is simply not available for a given referential category. How do speakers refer to what might be called "nonlexicalized categories"?

Examples of nonlexicalized categories can be expressed in phrases such as *things to take on a camping trip* or *places to look for antique desks.* These are examples of what Barsalou (1983: 211) has called "ad hoc" categories which are "often created spontaneously for use in specialized contexts." In contrast to common, lexicalized categories, these "ad hoc" categories tend to be less familiar and less central to cultural knowledge; they do not have well-established representations in memory; and they tend to serve people's goals rather than to represent states of the environment (Barsalou 1983).[5] Within an ad hoc category of this type, we may find a collection of members that otherwise have little in common: items as different as *a slipper, a newspaper, your foot,* and *a can of bug spray* all fit within the category *things to use to kill a roach.*

It is worth noting that the examples of ad hoc category labels suggested by Barsalou consist of nonspecific superordinate nouns (*things*) and infinitival purpose clauses (*to do X*). The linguistic structure of these category labels is appropriate for the expression of goal orientation, as emphasized in Barsalou's treatment. However, the spontaneous creation of a category, particularly one that is locally contingent, need not be expressed only in terms of a purpose or goal. In chapter 2, I noted the existence of phrases, such as *pine trees and stuff,* that can be used to accomplish category reference, not unlike the category label *evergreens.* However, there are many phrases with similar structures that do not seem to have a matching lexicalized category (encoded as a single lexicalized item). Consider the following examples.

[6]   (Donna and Julie are discussing their father's illness)
   1.   Donna: Maybe he has something like some kind of
      tumorous gro:wth **or something** in his—um they call it
      the retroperitoneum which is—(.) you have th—the
      peritoneum is a membrane that holds all th—your guts
      in, .hhh
   2.   Julie: Uh huh

[7]   (Sara wants Roger to talk to his landlord about letting
       her rent an apartment)
   1.   Sara: Tell 'em I don't have wild parties and throw
      people out windows **or whatever**
   2.   Roger: But you might be bri//nging a companion
   3.   Sara: Well I mi:ght.

[8]   (Crystal and Julie are talking about a mutual friend
       they had in high school)
   1.   Crystal: She had a weird family though. (1.0) Her
      brothers used to attack her 'n grab her boobs **'n stuff** 'n
   2.   Julie: O::h
   3.   Crystal: I think her father sexually molested her as a
      child.

The general extenders in the above examples appear to indicate nonlexicalized categories—"serious medical problems" in [6], "extremely irresponsible behaviors" in [7], and "sexual assaults" in [8]. It may be useful to think of common, lexicalized categories as representing one end of a continuum, and nonlexicalized categories as representing the other. The basis of this continuum is the degree to which the categories are (a) conventionally and linguistically established, and (b) constrained by contextual factors.[6]

Are general extenders more often used to implicate lexicalized or nonlexicalized categories? In my data, there are only six instances in which general extenders clearly implicate lexicalized categories. In the vast majority of instances (150), general extenders appear to implicate nonlexicalized categories. Why, then, are general extenders more frequently found to implicate nonlexicalized categories? An obvious explanation is that these expressions provide a way of talking about groups of entities or actions that spontaneously need to be referenced together when no established referring expression for the group is known (or even exists). As illustration, consider figure 3.5, a picture taken in Menstrie, Scotland. When a small shop stocks a novel collection of items, it is often difficult to represent what the store has

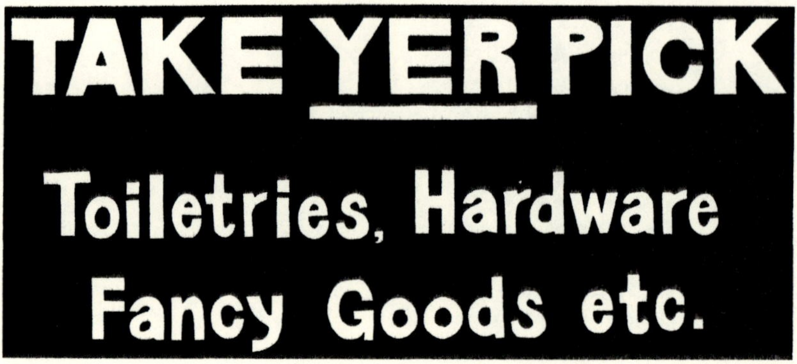

TAKE YER PICK

**Toiletries, Hardware
Fancy Goods etc.**

Figure 3.5. Store sign in Menstrie, Scotland.

to offer under a well-established, lexicalized label, such as *hard-ware* or *furniture*. Many shop-owners address this problem by listing some examples of the items sold, and indicating "more" with a general extender. In this case, the unusual collection of items sold includes toiletries, hardware, and fancy goods. The general extender *etc.* indicates that there is "more." In the chapters that follow, we will look at many more examples of general extenders used in connection with nonlexicalized categories.

Lexicalized Categories and General Extenders

With regard to the few instances in which a speaker uses a general extender to refer to a lexicalized category, an interesting question arises: Why would a speaker use a general extender to refer to a lexicalized category, when he or she could refer to the category by name? There are at least four possible reasons for this. First, by naming an item (or items), and then using a general extender to implicate a lexicalized category, a speaker can refer to a category whose name she either doesn't know, or can't recall.

Second, the speaker can identify members of a category for a hearer who may be unfamiliar with the category, or with its name. For example, consider, once again, the exchange in excerpt [9].

[9] 1. William: Are any of the uh trees turning?
     2. Julie: U:m they don't really turn much here I don't think.
     3. William: They don't
     4. Julie: Yeah.

5. William: Yeah. Most of 'em are evergreens around there I guess. Pine trees **an' stuff**.

In this case, William may suspect that Julie, who grew up in Hawai'i, is unfamiliar with the category *evergreens*. In addition to naming the lexicalized category, he provides an example (*pine trees*) in an effort to illustrate the kind of tree designated by this term.

Third, the speaker may use a general extender to emphasize the number of members in the category. This was illustrated in chapter 2, with the example repeated here as [10].

[10]   (Jean is speaking with her daughter, Julie)
1. Julie: You takin' a nap?
2. Jean: No:::=I've been (.) vacuumin' 'n (1.0) washin':
   (1.0) clo::thes 'n dustin': **'n: all that stuff**.
3. Julie: Umhm.

In responding to Julie's question in this manner, Jean creates a much longer response than if she were simply to name the category, and say "I've been doing *housework*." As noted in chapter 2, Jean's utterance in turn 2 might be seen to exhibit iconicity between message content (I have been doing a lot of work) and form (naming several instances of a category and creating a longer message, instead of simply naming the lexicalized category *housework*).

Finally, naming a specific example and indicating "more" with a general extender allows a speaker to emphasize or highlight certain members of the category. For example, as I leave the house on my way to the grocery store, I might say that *I'm going to get some milk, and stuff*. What I'm actually planning to get would be accurately described by the more general category label *groceries*. Choosing to say *milk and stuff* rather than *groceries* highlights one member of the category while also referring to the category. This focus on specific exemplars within a category may also be illustrated in excerpt [11], from a recorded conversation between two friends who are discussing hot-air ballooning. While looking through a newspaper, one of them says:

[11] I think it's in here there was a—an a:d. Maybe it's not
     in here. There've been a number of ads in these: uh::
     Cardinals and Badger Heralds **and things** lately—about—
     learning—about hot air ballooning from some sort of club.
     (Craig and Tracy 1983: 309)

The general extender *and things* in this context might be implicating other members of a category with the general label *newspapers*. The speaker chooses not to say *in the newspapers*, but names specific exemplars. One possible motivation for this might be a desire to draw attention to just these members within the larger category.

Although these four motivations suggest why general extenders may have a function in terms of lexicalized category implication, they actually explain only a very small portion of the data. As noted above, most general extenders appear to be used by speakers to implicate nonlexicalized categories. The next question, to be addressed in the following chapter, is how hearers interpret such uses.

–4–

Category Inference

By etcetera we mean that there are others, but not any others.

(Sacks 1992: 246)

The general picture to emerge from studies of category implication is one in which speakers attach a general extender (e.g., *and things*) to a named exemplar or exemplars (e.g., *forks*) to create an expression (e.g., *forks and things*) that implicates a category (e.g., *cutlery*). From this expression and its implication, the hearer can infer additional or alternate members (e.g., *spoons, knives*) of the category that the speaker has in mind. Stated in this way, with these particular examples, the category implication analysis seems to be a straight-forward and relatively simple way of accounting for general extenders and the cognitive processing involved in their interpretation. As I pointed out in chapter 3, however, there are serious problems with this simple version of what speakers and writers are doing when they use general extenders.

In this chapter I approach the issue from the perspective of what hearers (and readers) are doing when they interpret general extenders. I will continue to operate with the essentially psycholinguistic assumption that the cognitive process of categorization is crucially involved in the interpretation of general extenders. For example, I will look at how an expression such as *money orders, stamps, etc.* might best be interpreted on the basis of category inference. Among the questions to be addressed are: Is it feasible to assume that a hearer is able to infer the same category (or category members) that a speaker has in mind, based on the named items that precede a general extender? What factors help to constrain what a hearer may infer as potential members of a category? Or, using the words of Harvey Sacks in the quote above, how do we know what the "others" are?

Category Congruence

In chapter 3, we noted that speakers may indeed use general extenders to implicate additional or alternate instances of a category. However, there are some problems with the assumption that the named exemplars that precede a general extender will enable the hearer to infer the same category (or category members) that the speaker has in mind. Some problems with this proposal are summarized briefly in the following sections.

Named Exemplars and Prototypes

Following the experimental style of Rosch (1975), Channell (1994) set out to demonstrate that general extenders are used to identify categories. Phrases containing general extenders were presented to students who "were asked to list two or more items which they judged the speaker of each example 'could reasonably have been thinking of'" (Channell 1994: 124). In discussing her results, Channell proposed that "successful category identification" by a hearer (or reader) "necessitates giving a prototypical example of the intended category" (1994: 126). There are some obvious flaws in this approach to the analysis of general extenders,[1] and there is a serious problem with the concept of a prototype being assumed.

1. Categories do not appear to have fixed prototypes (Barsalou 1987, G. Lakoff 1987a, Neisser 1987). As noted in chapter 3, the structure of a category varies across both individuals and time. It follows that even if a speaker were to offer what she felt to be a prototypical exemplar, the hearer might not recognize it as such. As Channell observes, respondents in her experiment must have been using different "culturally defined categories" (1994: 127).

2. Although experimental tests have shown that people judge some items to be better examples of a category than others, this does not mean that categories are actually *represented* by these better examples, or prototypes. For example, if given a choice between the two, I might judge a *robin* to be a better example of *bird* than an *ostrich*. However, it is not necessarily the case that I have *robin* stored in memory as a representative example of the category *bird*. Both Rosch (1978) and G. Lakoff (1987b) have made this point.

3. Most, if not all, studies of prototypes have focused on the internal structure of lexicalized categories. To my knowledge, no studies have addressed the question of whether nonlexicalized categories

may have prototypes, and if so, what these prototypes might be. Because general extenders are most typically used to implicate non-lexicalized categories, a prototype-style analysis of the standard type cannot easily be applied in the majority of instances where general extenders are used.

Similarity as a Basis of Categorization

In discussions of the categorization approach, the hearer is generally presumed to infer additional or alternate instances of a category based on a notion of what is similar to the named exemplar(s). This is problematic for several reasons, including the following ones.

1. Similarity judgements may vary across individuals and time (see Murphy 1993, Shimron and Chernitsky 1995). For example, Murphy (1993: 185) has observed that "people with different levels of expertise have different patterns of similarity judgements, because of their theoretical sophistication," and he cites work by Chi, Feltovich, and Glaser (1981), and Murphy and Wright (1984) in support.

2. Similarity that is determined in terms of matching and mismatching properties depends on particular weights being given to specific properties. For example, "a skunk and a zebra would be more similar than a horse and a zebra if the feature 'striped' had sufficient weight" (Medin and Wattenmaker 1987: 27). In order to determine the relative weight given to a property, one must consider the larger context, not simply the named exemplars. Channell (1994: 128) notes that an exemplar such as a *car* was treated as similar to really diverse items, depending on which properties her respondents decided were salient. As a further illustration, consider the following two exchanges between Sara and Roger. In each exchange, Sara offers a sound made by her cat (*howl* in [1], and *yowl* in [2]) as a member of a category implicated by a general extender.

[1] 1. Sara: Y'know an' like uh (his emotional—) He was so good when I took him back to the v<u>e</u>t to have him l<u>oo</u>ked at?
  2. Roger: Oh, he didn't have to be sedated?
  3. Sara: No::, like, w—I mean, they just went an' sh— looked at him, she took his temperature, an' y'know stuck the thermometer up his butt, an' he didn't howl **or anything**. He didn't fi:::ght, or hiss, or scratch, or anything. He just kinda stoo:d the//re.
  4. Roger: Oh
  5. Sara: I was like "Cool!" I was so::: pleased.

[2] 1. Sara: My kitty is quiet. It's not like he sits in the
          window and yo̱:wls **or anything**
     2. Roger: There is one next door does that. Have you heard
          it?
     3. Sara: Um yea:h, actually . . .

Assuming that, for present purposes, there is no relevant difference
between the terms *howl* and *yowl*, the above examples may be seen to
show that the relative salience of an attribute varies according to
context. Whereas *howl* in [1] is a member of the category of "ways in
which the cat might have misbehaved at the vet," *yowl* in [2] is a
member of the category of "nonquiet cat noises." Whereas the locally
salient property of *howl* might be characterized as "unpleasant," the
locally salient property of *yowl* is "loud."

    3. As noted in chapter 3, the notion of similarity as a basis of
categorization has been questioned by many scholars (cf. Medin 1989,
Murphy and Medin 1985, Rips 1989, Spaulding and Murphy 1996,
Tversky 1977). Recent research has drawn attention to the fact that
categories have a more complex source than that of perceptual similarity (cf. Gelman et al. 1994, Keil 1991, Medin 1989).

Categories as Consisting of Perceivable Objects

    Previous studies have focused primarily on categories consisting
of first-order entities (e.g., physical objects). However, general
extenders often appear to be conjoined with second-order entities (e.g.,
events, processes, or states), and with third-order entities (e.g.,
abstract entities outside space and time, such as propositions). In fact,
there is a crucial difference in the ontological status of these entity
types which is relevant to our consideration of the category-style
analysis. According to Lyons, first-order entities are less controversial
than second- and third-order entities, because it is characteristic that
"they are relatively constant as to their perceptual properties; that
they are located, at any point in time, in what is, psychologically at
least, a three-dimensional space; and that they are publicly observable" (1977: 43). Since second- and third-order entities are less objectively perceivable than first-order entities, it follows that the categorization of these entities would rely more heavily on subjective
conceptualization. It seems reasonable to expect that where categories consist of second- or third-order entities, variation among individuals' categories would be more pronounced, and that the inference
of (the same) additional or alternate instances would be problematic.

    Based on these observations, it seems unlikely that a hearer can
infer the same category (or category members) that a speaker has in
mind, based simply on the named exemplars that precede a general

extender. What other factors might help a hearer to infer additional or alternate instances that may be indicated by a general extender? The answer to this question lies not in the phrase containing the general extender, but in the larger context of its occurrence.

Contextual Constraints

In the discussion of categorization in chapter 3, I noted that the range of items that might be included in a category is constrained by contextual factors. In this section, I will present some empirically observable examples of constraints imposed by linguistic context (i.e., cotext), the broader context, and background knowledge.

The Linguistic Context

The interpretation of a general extender is often constrained, in part, by the speaker's subsequent discourse. In such cases, the speaker may either describe or name the category, or identify relevant similarities among its members (e.g., properties or functions). For example, consider excerpt [3].

[3]   (Maya is talking to Sara about a mutual friend of
       theirs, Wendy, and her sadistic treatment of animals;
       Wendy has just had her dog put to sleep.)
       Maya: I don't think she believes that they'll like (.)
       bleed an' stuff. I don't think she understands that (.)
       when she gassed her dog that the dog bloated and lost
       oxygen and choked to death and (.) twitched and then
       died you know. I think she thinks they (.) put it in a I
       dunno Vegematic **or something** and just kind of pureed it
       and poured it outside. I don't know. Or took the battery
       out. I don't know.

The point of interest in [3] is where Maya says: *I think she thinks they (.) put it in a I dunno Vegematic or something and just kind of pureed it and poured it outside.* In this example, the phrase that follows the general extender *or something* identifies the relevant function of the named member (i.e., *a Vegematic*) as being something capable of liquefying solid material. Thus, all members of the category implicated by *or something* would be capable of this function.

Although it appears to be relatively uncommon (there are only two examples in my data set), general extenders are sometimes further specified by a subsequent relative clause, as in excerpts [4]–[5].

[4]   Maya: My nose ru:ns and (.) my eyeballs oo:ze an' (.) **things like that that aren't real attractive**.

[5]   Donna: You know what um do you have a bucket **or anything** I can wash the cat in?

Excerpts [6]–[7], from newspaper articles, contain further examples of this pattern:

[6]   (Article on Alzheimer's disease)
       "Underneath all of us there is a lot of angst, and sometimes we're willing to say what's going on, to tell the truth. We have fears, you know. We're all afraid the day will come when they have to put us in a box, **or whatever they do with people who can't think or speak anymore**." —Frank McShane, Alzheimer's patient. (*Baton Rouge Advocate*, 4 June 1995)

[7]   (Review article evaluating a new photo documentary book)
       And I think that's pretty amazing—to present these images in a way that says, "Here are my folks, poor sad monsters that they are," and not add a "AND YOU MADE THEM THIS WAY!" or "AND THEY MADE ME THIS WAY," **or any of that whiny crap that's so often mistaken for what makes photography like this "important," or, worse, "courageous."** (*New York Press*, 12–18 June 1996)

A final example comes from the Bible:

[8]   Neither shall you covet your neighbor's house, or field, or male or female slave, or ox, or donkey, **or anything that belongs to your neighbor.** (*Deuteronomy* 5: 6–21)

In these further specified instances, the relative clause helps to constrain the interpretation of the category implicated by the general extender by naming the category (*whatever they do with people who can't think or speak anymore* in [6], *whiny crap that's so often mistaken for what makes photography like this "important," or, worse, "courageous"* in [7], *anything that belongs to your neighbor* in [8]), or by identifying either characteristic properties of its members (*aren't real attractive* in [4]), or their common function (*I can wash the cat in* in [5]). We might refer to these instances as "specific extenders" to differentiate them from "general extenders," which are necessarily non-specific.

Another way in which the interpretation of a general extender can be constrained by linguistic context is illustrated in excerpts [9]–[11]. In each of these excerpts, the speaker uses the general extender within a structure that not only expresses what something *is*, but additionally what it *is not*.

[9]   (Article on Harrison Ford, who plays Jack Ryan in the
      movie Clear and Present Danger)
      Although Ryan is often surrounded by explosions and
      gunfire, Ford says he never puts himself in any real danger.
      "I don't do stunts," he says. "I do running, jumping, falling
      down. I hit people, I get hit by people, **that kind of shit.**
      Stunts are done by stuntmen."(*Entertainment Weekly*,
      Summer 1994)

[10] Sara: My kitty is quiet. It's not like he sits in the window
      and y<u>ow</u>:ls **or anything**

[11]   (Roger is in Hawai'i, and Sara is in Louisiana)
      1. Roger: you hike to grea:t looking places h<u>e</u>re.
      2. Sara: Yea::h
      3. Roger: An' at the // end of the hike you
      4. Sara: heh hah hah hah Not like hiking up near like
          the Lousiana State Penitentiary **or anyth//ing**
      5. Roger: Na::h. No::, it's like you hike to a w<u>a</u>terfall
          here,
      6. Sara: hhh.
      7. Roger: an' at the bottom of the waterfall there's a pool,
          an' you .hh // di::ve i::n
      8. Sara: (sploosh) right on in

As Frake (1969: 36) points out, to define a category, one must know not just what it includes, but what it contrasts with. By setting up a contrast, the speakers in excerpts [9]-[11] identify features that are *not* characteristic of the category (or members of the category) implicated by the use of a general extender. For example, in [9], the kinds of actions performed by Harrison Ford—running, jumping, falling down, and exchanging blows—are members of the category implicated by the general extender. This category is contrasted with *stunts*, which are considered more dangerous. The actions performed by Ford are thereby designated as a category of *non-stunts* which are to be interpreted as *not dangerous*. In [10], Sara says, *My kitty is quiet. It's not like he sits in the window and yowls or anything*. Here *yowls* may be viewed as a member of a category of "non-quiet kitty behaviors."

Finally, in [11], Sara's *Not like hiking up near the Louisiana State Penitentiary or anything*, in turn 13, is contrasted with Roger's *you hike to grea:t looking places here*. In other words, the Louisiana State Penitentiary is a member of a category of "not-great-looking places near which to hike."

Excerpts [12] and [13], from other data sources, further demonstrate how contrast can be used to define these locally contingent categories. In [12], an Iraqi opposition figure is expressing his surprise at the way in which Saddam Hussein's son-in-law was murdered.

[12] I just didn't expect it to be done so quickly or so brutally . . .
      I thought some poison in his drink **or something like that** a
      few weeks down the road would kill him. (*New York
      Times*, 25 Feb. 1996)

In this extract, the speaker remarks that the murder was performed *so quickly and so brutally*, and that he did not expect it to be done that way. Instead, he expected *some poison in his drink or something like that a few weeks down the road*. Here, *some poison in his drink* is offered as a member of a category of "non-brutal ways to kill someone." In [13], a surfer is talking about his friend's death in twenty-foot surf at Waimea Bay, in Hawai'i.

[13] I'm glad for him. I'm sure all surfers would rather go this
      way than in a car accident **or something**. (*Honolulu
      Advertiser*, 24 Dec. 1995)

In this case, the speaker contrasts dying in big surf with a category of ways to die that include *in a car accident*. Even though he does not specify how dying in big surf is different from dying in a car accident, we might infer that the latter represents a category of common and relatively uninteresting ways to die.[2]

An examination of naturally occurring, interactive data reveals that the relevant category implicated by a general extender is sometimes negotiated via the hearer's interpretation, and the speaker's subsequent acceptance of that interpretation. For example, in each of the following two excerpts, the general extender occurs in a yes/no question. In answering the question in the negative, the hearer produces an observable interpretation of what is *not* included in the category implicated by the speaker's use of a general extender.

[14]   (Joy is inquiring about a small town in Louisiana that
          Roger is familiar with)
      1. Joy: An' like do you like go up there on weekends
          sometimes or // do they
      2. Roger: .hh I have—

3. Joy: have good restaurants **an' stuff**?
4. Roger: No, no.
5. Joy: Oh
6. Roger: They don't have good restaurants. They have funky little places to eat.
7. Joy: Uh huh

[15]   (Excerpts of 911 Records appearing in article on O. J. Simpson case)
1. Nicole: Well, my ex-husband—or my husband—just broke in . . . and he's ranting and raving.
2. Operator: Has he been drinking **or anything**?
3. Nicole: No, but he's crazy.
4. Operator: Did he hit you?
5. Nicole: No. (*Newsweek*, 4 July 1994)

In turns 1 and 3 of excerpt [14], Joy asks Roger *do they have good restaurants and stuff?*; Roger responds with *No no* in turn 4, and then elaborates on his answer in turn 6: *They don't have good restaurants. They have funky little places to eat.* Roger's answer reveals that his interpretation of the category implicated by the general extender in the phrase *good restaurants and stuff* (if, in fact, a category is implicated at all) does not include *funky little places to eat*. The fact that Joy does not reject Roger's interpretation in line 7, but utters *uh huh*, can be taken as evidence that she accepts it.

A similar phenomenon is found in excerpt [15]. In turn 2, the operator asks Nicole *Has he been drinking or anything?*; Nicole replies *No, but he's crazy*. Nicole's answer demonstrates that her interpretation of the category implicated by the general extender in the phrase *drinking or anything* does not include *crazy*. (Nicole's use of the logical connector *but* may indicate, however, that he was exhibiting behavior that she associates with substance abuse.) The fact that the operator moves to another question in turn 4, and does not challenge Nicole's interpretation, can be seen as evidence that she accepts it. An important observation with regard to excerpts [14] and [15] is that the interpretation of general extenders is negotiated by the participants, and it is interactionally specified. Some further examples and a discussion of this will be presented in chapter 5.

The Broader Context

Examples [3]–[15] illustrate how empirically observable aspects of the linguistic context may serve to constrain the analysis of general extenders. However, much of what limits the interpretation of these

expressions cannot be located within the co-text. Instead, the interpretation of the general extender is constrained by a broader context.
As illustration, consider the following. During a visit to Albertson's
grocery store in Baton Rouge, I noticed a sign posted at a service
counter with two windows. The left side of the sign had an arrow
pointing to the left window and read *Money orders, Stamps, etc.*; the
right side of the sign had an arrow pointing to the right window and
read *Lotto*. This sign is reproduced as figure 4.1. Looking only at the
left side of the notice, think of what would be interpreted as part of
etc. if only the co-text of *Money Orders, Stamps,* were available. Is a
particular category implicated?

In this particular instance, *etc.* actually referred to everything
except Lotto (lottery tickets) that a customer might seek at the
service counter in this particular store (e.g., to buy newspapers, make
inquiries, or request refunds). It is interesting to note that the referenced category implicated by *etc.* in this case is defined both by
contrast with the other part of the sign (everything except Lotto) and
by a kind of contiguity, in that the members are things that are
handled in the same location. In fact, the members of the category
may not actually be "similar" in any way. In such instances, unless
they are familiar with the particular store, hearers (or readers) may
not be able to infer any additional instances that may be implicated
by the general extender *etc.*

Figure 4.1. Sign in grocery store.

This is a Septic System

Please do not place
Sanitary Napkins etc.
in the toilet
Please use the Bin
~ provided ~

Figure 4.2. Sign in pub in Sherrifmuir, Scotland.

Now consider a second example. While enjoying some Guinness at a pub in Sheriffmuir, Scotland, I took a trip to the bathroom, where I saw the sign that appears as figure 4.2. In order to infer any additional items which might be indicated by the general extender *etc.* in this case, I had to consider the setting (bathroom), as well as the purpose of the message (i.e., what the sign-maker intended to come about—or not—as a result of this communication). Assuming that the sign-maker hoped to avoid the unpleasant experience of a clogged toilet or malfunctioning septic system, I inferred that the category of items I wasn't supposed to put in the toilet included other bulky items that women might wish to dispose of in this setting, such as tampons, paper towels, and nappies (diapers).

Background Knowledge

In order to proceed in the analysis of the participants' interpretation of general extenders, we must assume, as the participants do, that certain assumptions about background knowledge will be taken for granted. The following examples illustrate how assumed background knowledge may constrain the interpretation of a general extender.

The first example comes from an interview with Calvert DeForest in *People* magazine (17 Jan. 1994). In reference to a picture of him as a young man in 1951, DeForest said *This is when my hair was dark and everything.* Here, an interpretation of the additional instances implicated by *and everything* might include any of the things that are associated with a youthful appearance. In this interpretation, the ability to infer the additional instances depends on a knowledge of what younger people typically look like.

In [16], the speaker is telling a story about a time when she and her friends were interrogated at the Los Angeles airport about luggage containing psilocybin ("magic") mushrooms.

[16] I guess (.) somebody (.) in tryin' ta decide what the hell
      these things are had picked up (.) some of the mushrooms
      an' went an' went ta smell it (.) an' he got—he had cow shit
      (2) he didn't pick a piece a mushroom he picked a piece a
      cow shit up (laughs) he was—he was not happy 'cuz he
      had cow shit all over his hands an' on his nose **an' stuff** (.)
      so he was (.) I mean it was real intresting. but they let us go
      an' gave us the suitcase. (Guthrie 1994: 88)

In this instance, the hearer's interpretation of the general extender in the phrase *he had cow shit all over his hands an' on his nose an' stuff*, would be constrained, at least in part, by the knowledge of what is involved in the action of smelling. The customs agent would have picked up the cow shit with one or two hands and raised it to his nose. Based on this assumed knowledge, the hearer would most likely infer that, in addition to getting it on his hands and his nose, the agent may have gotten it on other areas of his body near his hands or nose (e.g., his upper lip, his forearm), or possibly dropped some and gotten it on his shoe. The hearer would probably *not* infer that he had gotten it on his back, his ear, or the top of his head. In such a case, the interpretation required for the general extender *an' stuff* clearly depends on what Miller (1978) called practical, rather than lexical, knowledge.

It is important to note that, despite the apparently inexplicit nature of these expressions, participants treat their interpretation as unproblematic. Speakers using general extenders assume that hearers will be able to supply "whatever unstated understandings are required" (Garfinkel 1967: 3) to make recognizable sense of the speaker's talk, and hearers typically exhibit no difficulty in interpreting them.[3]

The *And So Forth* Idealization

It seems reasonable to assume that the interpretation of just about any utterance will depend on the assumption of some type of shared knowledge. Along these lines, Garfinkel's (1967: 38–41) conversation clarification experiment showed that in two-party conversations, "much that is being talked about is not mentioned, although each expects that the adequate sense of the matter being talked about is settled" (Garfinkel 1963: 221; see also Heritage 1984: 81). Researchers since Bartlett (1932) have proposed that schemata, or pre-existing knowledge structures such as scripts (dynamic event sequences) and frames (fixed representations), function as familiar patterns from previous experience, and that these patterns enable participants to arrive at interpretations of the unsaid (see Schank and Abelson 1977, Minsky 1975). This process is described by Schutz and Luckmann as follows:

> Each step of my interpretation of the world is based at any given time on a stock of previous experience: my own direct experiences, as well as such experiences as are conveyed to me by my fellow-men, above all by my parents, teachers, etc. All of these conveyed and direct experiences merge to form a unified stock of knowledge, which serves me as a reference schema for the immediate step of my interpretation of the world. All of my experiences of the life-world are brought in relation to this schema, so that the objects and events in the life-world confront me from the outset in their typical character. . . . Every interpretation within the life-world is an interpretation within a frame of that which has already been interpreted, within a reality that is fundamentally and typically familiar. I trust that the world as it has been known by me up until now will continue to be as it is, and that consequently the stock of knowledge obtained from my fellow-men and formed from my own experiences will continue to preserve its fundamental validity.[4] (1977: 29)

I have included this extensive quotation because it is tied to a way of thinking about knowledge interpretation that is very relevant to the current investigation. In writing about the assumption that the structure of the world is constant, and that the stock of knowledge one has will remain valid, Schutz and Luckmann (1977, 1984) use an expression from Husserl's work (1929/1977: 41–42) to label it the *Idealität des Und So Weiter*, or the And So Forth Idealization. The And So Forth Idealization seems to correspond to the notion that "categorization, in essence, is a device for treating a new experience as though it were something familiar" (Frake 1969: 36; see also Bruner et al. 1956).

The choice of the descriptive label *and so forth*, as well as the general characterization of the interpretation associated with it, represent a clear precedent for my proposal that an assumption of shared experience must play a crucial role in the function of general extenders. This point will receive further attention in chapter 5.

Limitations of Category-Style Approaches and the Psycholinguistic Perspective

In chapters 3 and 4, I have considered the most common responses of analysts to the function of general extenders. Those responses have been absorbed with an attempt to work out how general extenders function referentially, and how they contribute to the content of messages. The general conclusion has been that, in combination with named exemplars, they implicate categories. The underlying assumption is that general extenders are signals to a cognitive processing mechanism that uses the attached exemplar(s) as the basis for identifying a general category, thus triggering the recognition of additional category members. The psycholinguistic perspective involved in this type of analysis provided many insights into how speakers (or writers) might use the assumption of category inference by their listeners (or readers) when they construct their referring expressions. However, we have noted some problems with this perspective and the type of data typically employed in claims about how general extenders function. An important observation made in this chapter is that, while context and background knowledge often help to constrain a hearer's interpretation, it is unlikely that these factors enable a hearer to infer some specific category (or category members) that a speaker has in mind.

In fact, we might question the underlying assumption that a speaker necessarily has additional or alternate instances of some category in mind when using a general extender. Although some rare perspicuous cases (such as examples [1]–[5] in chapter 3) seem to demonstrate that speakers do this, on some occasions it seems that general extenders are employed simply to indicate the *potential* existence of other instances. In such cases, if pressed by the hearer, a speaker might not be in a position to name any others at all (this interesting possibility will be considered in chapter 8).

Perhaps a more significant question is whether general extenders necessarily implicate categories at all. It appears often they do not. In his study of a Scottish dialect, Macaulay (1991: 171) notes the frequent occurrence of general extenders in an interview with one speaker. Macaulay reports that while some instances may be interpreted as category or set-marking, "the great majority" of general extenders in his data "are much harder to interpret as in any way set-marking." He offers the following examples in support of this claim:

[17] if I had her cleaned up **and that**

[18] aye but it—it was a cheap holiday **and that**

[19] I didn't feel it tight **and that**

[20] when he died **and that**

Examples like these suggest that general extenders do not necessarily function referentially or contribute to the content of messages. (Similar examples will be analyzed more closely in chapter 7.)

Finally, there is a much more serious limitation that characterizes the category-style approach to general extenders. The psycholinguistic bias of the approach has led to the almost complete exclusion of sociolinguistic considerations in the analysis. General extenders have been analyzed as if they existed in a social vacuum. Given their most frequent occurrence in interpersonal talk among familiars, it seems unlikely that general extenders have no sociolinguistic role.

From this review of what hearers seem to be expected to do to arrive at an interpretation of a general extender, we can now see that a purely ideational approach to the analysis of general extenders is not the answer. In order to provide an accurate account of how general extenders are employed by language users in actual contexts, we must broaden our field of analysis, beginning in chapter 5, to consider their function in interpersonal terms.

PART THREE

Interpersonal Function

–5–

Intersubjectivity

Y'know, she wants whales, candlelight, and stuff like that.

There are occasions in the analysis of spoken interactional discourse among familiars when the meanings apparently recognized and shared by the participants seem to be unfathomable to anyone else. What the speaker of the quote above had in mind when she used the expression *and stuff like that* may be guessed at by an outside observer, but it is unlikely ever to match what her familiar interlocutor was assumed to understand by what was said. I will return to this example in the course of this chapter, as I attempt to explore the strongly interpersonal function of general extenders.

In chapters 3 and 4, the focus of investigation was the possibility of analyzing general extenders in terms of categories. In many cases, it appears to be quite feasible to think of potential categories that may be implicated by an occurrence of a general extender. Indeed, in almost all examples cited out of context, it is possible for the analyst to propose a likely category as referent for a general extender. However, as I hope to illustrate in the remaining chapters, within their actual contexts of occurrence, general extenders do not appear to be used with category implication as their most obvious function. Rather, when viewed in terms of their role within the interactive exchange of talk, general extenders appear to have a function that is interpersonal and tied to the nature of the participants' social relationships. Consequently, the discussion will now shift from a concern with the cognitive and the categorial to an exploration of the interpersonal role of general extenders. The relevant conceptual background will also naturally shift from the psycholinguistic to the sociolinguistic.

In this chapter, I will explore how, in using a general extender, a speaker marks an assumption of shared knowledge and experience with the hearer, thereby underscoring an assumed closeness. Where the participants are not already socially close, these forms represent an implicit appeal to move closer. A concept crucial to this discussion is that of intersubjectivity.

Defining Intersubjectivity

In chapters 3 and 4, consideration was given to the proposal that in using a general extender, a speaker implicates a category, so that a hearer can infer additional or alternate members of the category the speaker has in mind. In this picture, a speaker's intended category is assumed to match the hearer's inferred category in an objective way; the participants' worlds are being treated as identical at some categorial level. This, in principle, would be a very misleading perspective from which to consider interactive talk. A great deal of philosophical writing has been devoted to exploring the notion that individual mental worlds are necessarily distinct. The real focus of interest is how humans manage to create comparability of categories, or even sufficient overlap, given the assumption of non-identical worlds. This process has been described in terms of intersubjectivity.

Contemporary discussions of intersubjectivity focus on how participants can reach similar interpretations, and they ascribe this achievement to an assumption of shared knowledge, or a co-conception of the world (see Schegloff 1992; Schiffrin 1990, 1994a). The roots of this approach to an assumed co-conception of the world can be found, in different manifestations, in the work of Cicourel (1974), Durkheim (1915), Garfinkel (1967), Husserl (1929/1977), Mead (1938), and Schutz (1932/1967).

For Husserl, a philosopher writing in the late nineteenth and early twentieth centuries, it was important to draw a distinction between individual subjective experience and the assumed existence of a world beyond, and independent of, that individual subjectivity:

> First of all, before everything else conceivable, I am. This "I am" is for me, the subject who says it, and says it in the right sense, the primitive intentional basis for my world; at the same time, I may not overlook that the "objective" world, the "world for all of us" as accepted with this sense by me, is also "my" world. "I am" is the primitive intentional basis, however, not only for "the" world, that I consider real, but also for any "ideal world" that I accept; for everything that I hold to exist—sometimes legitimately,

sometimes illegitimately, etc.—including myself, my life, my believing, all this consciousness.[1] (1929/1977: 89-90)

Given that our conceptualization of the world is necessarily subjective, it seems reasonable to assume that no two individuals will share identical concepts. In fact, many analysts proceed as if it is simply not the case that separate minds have identical contents (see Garfinkel 1967, Schegloff 1992). It follows that, in principle, even if a speaker had a specific category in mind when using a general extender as a category implicative expression, the hearer's inferred category would, in many cases, not exactly match the speaker's intended category. I have already explored some aspects of this issue in the preceding chapter. It has also been noted in the work of Barsalou (1983), Frake (1969), and Dougherty (1981), on categorization.

Despite the fact that individual conceptualizations of the world necessarily differ, social actors typically assume shared knowledge and a shared world (Husserl 1929/1977: 92), and they behave as if the external world is sufficiently the same for them as it is for others. Before the term "intersubjectivity" came into general use, this aspect of human interactive behavior was described in terms of a "reciprocity of perspectives" (see Cicourel 1974, Schegloff 1992, Schutz 1962, Schutz and Luckmann 1977). Contemporary writers on this topic generally credit Schutz with the original articulation of this crucial insight. Heritage summarizes Schutz's observations in the following way:

> Actors engaged in coordinated actions with others will assume the socially standardized and shared nature of their knowledge and will seek actively, if unconsciously, to sustain it. They will accomplish this by maintaining the "reciprocity of perspectives"—subject only to the provision that they assume that knowledge arising from their own particular biographical circumstances will be available to others only to a limited extent, which is, partially at least, under the autonomous control of each individual. (1984: 77)

The "reciprocity of perspectives" described above is the procedure through which intersubjectivity is achieved (Schegloff 1992: 1297). According to Cicourel, Schutz's reciprocity of perspectives is an "interpretive procedure basic to all interaction," which consists of two parts:

> The first part instructs the speaker and hearer to assume their mutual experiences of the interaction are the same

even if they were to change places. The second part informs
each participant to disregard personal differences in how
each assigns meaning to everyday activities, thus each can
attend the present scene in an identical manner for the
practical matter at hand. (1974: 34)

Given this general operational basis for social interaction, it
would not be surprising if interactive talk contained expressions that
were conventionally used to invoke an assumption of shared experience or intersubjectivity. One of the most easily recognizable of such
expressions is *you know what I mean*, or simply *you know*. I would like
to suggest that general extenders are used to fulfill a similar broad
function. In using a general extender, the speaker communicates the
following message to the hearer: "Because we share the same knowledge, experience, and conceptual schemes, I do not need to be explicit;
you will be able to supply whatever unstated understandings are required to make sense of the utterance." Functioning in this way, general extenders are recognizable indications that all talk is, in some
sense, incomplete (see Garfinkel 1967), and that each of us expects our
interactive partners to collaborate in creating whatever sense of com-
pleteness is sufficient for a particular occasion.

Highly transparent examples of this process are not hard to find.
In [1], the speaker is reported to have used the expression *you name it*,
directly inviting his listeners to recognize other security issues as
shared knowledge.

[1]   (article on the United States' role in Bosnia)
       Oddly enough, Secretary of State Warren Christopher
       sounded much the same theme on Friday, saying: "Our
       nation's ability to work with these European countries on
       every other security issue—reducing the nuclear threat,
       fighting terrorism, **you name it**—depends on our
       partnership here." (*New York Times*, 10 Dec. 1995)

The use of *you name it* signals, in a quite literal way, the speaker's
assumption that the listener is able to name other examples of this
type.

Shared Knowledge and Experience

The realization that general extenders may mark an assumption of
shared knowledge or reciprocal perspectives creates an inherent problem for their interpretation by a non-participant (e.g., the analyst) in
an interaction. The analyst is constantly faced with the task of recon-
structing what might be assumed in an intersubjective world created

by others. The type of knowledge required to infer what may be implicated by the use of a general extender ranges along a continuum from broad, cultural, or general knowledge potentially shared by many, to knowledge that is shared only by a small number of interactional participants. For example, in [2], Sara and Maya are talking about a mutual friend who is planning to move to another state. In order to infer what is implicated by the general extender *or anything like that* in [2], Sara may be assumed to recognize the named items, *call me* and *write me*, as ways that members of her culture keep in touch.

[2] 1. Maya: I really think as soon as she moves to
          Connecticut I won't know her anymore. I'm sure she's not
          gonna call me or you know write me **or anything like
          th//at.**
     2. Sara: I have a feeling she's gonna—sh—I'm not gonna
          know her much anymore either

The conventional set of "ways of keeping in touch" may qualify as a kind of broad or general knowledge that the analyst, as a non-participant in the interaction, can attribute to the participants.

A second example of this is offered in [3]. In this excerpt from the novel *Heartburn*, the writer appeals to what may be viewed as a type of general knowledge, by citing a common saying:

[3] I've always liked odd and interesting-looking men because
     I'm odd and interesting-looking myself, and I always
     figured I had a better shot at them than at the
     conventionally good-looking ones. (Water seeks its own
     level, **et cetera**.) (Ephron 1983: 70-71)

The speaker is appealing to the kind of general knowledge encoded in clichés and well-known sayings as a way of making sense of how she behaves. Based on this type of example, we might say that cultural sayings such as *water seeks its own level* can be considered a kind of broad or generally shared knowledge that the analyst can attribute to the participants (in this case, writer and readers). However, the analyst may not always have such an easy task.

Sometimes, a speaker or writer assumes a less common form of knowledge, that is shared by a smaller subgroup of the culture. Consider excerpt [4].

[4] If you wanna hear Madonna, Whitney, Janet, **etc.** go next
     door!

This example is taken from a sign in front of a deejay's booth in a pub and pool hall that adjoins a gay bar in Honolulu. In order to understand the function of the general extender *etc.* here, one needs to know something about the kind of music that is typically played in gay bars, as an extension of that associated with *Madonna, Whitney [Houston]*, and *Janet [Jackson]*. Note that while it may be difficult for an individual unfamiliar with gay culture to understand this sign, there are still a relatively large number of individuals who would be able to make sense of it, based on shared knowledge.

As we move toward the far end of this continuum, there are certain occasions when the knowledge shared between participants seems completely inaccessible to non-participants. In a discussion of "the architecture of intersubjectivity," Rommetveit (1974: 29) notes how "similar states of nearly perfect complementarity and synchronization of intentions and thoughts" may result in conversations that are cryptic to outsiders but are perfectly understood by the participants. Since the interpretation of an interpersonally established, potentially private way of seeing the world depends on having access to some specialized knowledge shared by the participants, it is difficult for an analyst, as an outsider, to be certain that any interpretation of interactive data involving others will match that of the participants. As illustration of this point, the following example, reconstructed from a personal (non-recorded) conversation, is offered to demonstrate a speaker's use of a general extender to implicate a certain kind of private knowledge.

[5]   (George and Mary are talking about their friends,
         Dexter and Charlene)
   1. Mary: Charlene is really unhappy with Dexter.
   2. George: Why?
   3. Mary: Y'know, she wants whales, candlelight, **and
       stuff like that**.

A stranger overhearing the exchange in [5] would likely experience difficulty in identifying what Mary has in mind. After all, *whales* and *candlelight* are not typically thought of as members of a conventional category, and Mary does not elaborate on what the *stuff like that* might be. In order to determine with any certainty what Mary is referring to, the stranger would need access to knowledge or experience that Mary shares with George. Only then might the stranger recognize what I (the speaker) had in mind: that Charlene wants to share certain kinds of experiences with Dexter and have him enjoy those experiences in the way that George and I share and enjoy the experiences associated with the terms mentioned prior to the general extender. In particular, George and I spend long periods of free time together on whale-watching trips to the coast and share a certain awe at the sight of those amazing creatures. We also spend time together making and eating dinner at home by candlelight. I can assume that, on the basis of these shared experiences, George can arrive at a general intersubjective understanding of what I mean by *whales, candlelight, and stuff like that*. We could simply label this as a category of "romantic things," but this label would be a massively underspecified representation of what is intersubjectively understood in this case.

Problems with "Empirical" Testing

An obvious question arises at this point: Why not perform some experimental tests to ascertain how non-participants interpret utterances containing general extenders? In fact, this has already been attempted by Channell. As noted in chapter 4, Channell (1994: 124) presented phrases containing general extenders to students who "were asked to list two or more items which they judged the speaker of each example 'could reasonably have been thinking of'" when he or she used a general extender. Even where examples seemed to invoke a broadly shared type of cultural knowledge, the thirty-nine respondents came up with a very large number of potential interpretations. For example, given the utterance *They've got a car and that*, the students listed more than fifty possible items, including some as diverse as a *canoe, two toilets*, a *mortgage*, and a *decent-looking garden*. Among the many items named, there was little overlap: thirty-seven of the items were mentioned only once. We must assume that the individual participant in the interaction who heard the general extender *and that* in this case did not have all these items come to mind.

Channell's test results suggest that what is intersubjectively understood by the use of a general extender is not easily isolated from the participants or its context of occurrence. Without knowing the participants, having access to their shared knowledge, and being familiar with the context of utterance, the non-participant analyst is able only to guess at what might be intersubjectively understood by participants.

The Co-construction of Intersubjectivity

Intersubjective understanding also appears frequently to be co-constructed in the course of an interaction, and it often seems to be dependent on the activation of shared experiential knowledge. As illustration, the following extract involves Crystal and Julie, both in their thirties, who have been friends since high school and, during a phone conversation, are catching up on recent personal news. In [6], Crystal is describing some of her new friends to Julie.

[6] 1. Crystal: I been—I've sort of found some f—different
         kind of friends um th//at I've been hanging out with
     2. Julie: That's good.
     3. Crystal: Yeah. (.) So I—girlfriends, y'know, which is
         good for me. They stay out late, too, so I always bump
         into 'em. They're like (.) strippers 'n // huh huh
     4. Julie: Mmhm
     5. Crystal: So we'll like meet after work, an' have
         cocktails, an' dance, 'n just go flirt with the boys, so—
     6. Julie: heh // heh
     7. Crystal: We have fu::n.
     8. Julie: Strippers, huh?
     9. Crystal: Oh, it's funny. But they're totally ni::ce //
         y'know
    10. Julie: Uh huh
    11. Crystal: an' this one girl you would not even know it.
         She looks like she works in a grocery store **or
         something**. Y'know. Just totally normal // an'
    12. Julie: conservative
    13. Crystal: Yeah, yeah. She just—She's young, and she
         likes to travel, an' she's just having fun with it,
    14. Julie: Umhm
    15. Crystal: an' um they're totally cool.

The point of interest in this excerpt is in turn 11, where Crystal describes one of the strippers she has been hanging out with. Crystal says that the girl *looks like she works in a grocery store or something*. She then elaborates on the expression containing the general extender with *y'know, just totally normal*. Here Crystal appears to use *a grocery store* as an example of a place where normal people work. By indicating "places where normal people work," Crystal demonstrates an expectation that Julie will recognize and share her personal concept of what kind of person works at a grocery store. Indeed, Julie demonstrates acceptance of the concept by offering a further characterization of such a person as being *conservative*. This contribution is approved by Crystal, who replies *yeah, yeah*.

Regardless of whether the implicated concept is culturally established (e.g., ways to keep in touch with someone) or more novel (e.g., places where the participants think "normal" people work), the basic function of the general extender is the same. In using a general extender, the speaker conveys to the hearer an assumption of shared knowledge, and she invites the hearer to supply whatever unstated understandings are required to make sense of the utterance. By demonstrating an assumption of shared knowledge with the hearer in this manner, the speaker underscores a similarity between the participants. This can be seen either to reaffirm existing familiarity, or to represent a bid to decrease social distance. In turn, by treating the speaker's utterance as unproblematic (and disregarding personal differences in how each assigns meaning to everyday activities), the hearer reciprocally underscores the participants' similarity. General extenders do not implicate categories as much as they implicate intersubjectivity.

Support for this perspective is provided by those occasional examples of general extender use in a context where participants do not actually have first-hand knowledge or experience of what is assumed, yet they indicate that they understand. For example, consider the following exchange between the same two women who were talking in example [6], and who used to party together in high school.

[7]   (Crystal has just told Julie that she tried a new
        recreational drug, called Ecstasy, or "E")
  1. Julie: Oh, wo:w, how was that?
  2. Crystal: That was fun. It was fun.
  3. Julie: I've been curious about that. John knows people
     who've taken that.
  4. Crystal: It's kind of like—It's just like really mild
     acid.
  5. Julie: Oh, is th<u>a</u>t what it is?
  6. Crystal: Mmhm. That's what I felt. That's what it
     made me feel, y'know just the .hh colors an' the (2.0)
     y'know uh the way it makes you thi:nk an' (.) **stuff.**
  7. Julie: Mmh//m
  8. Crystal: Except it made—it makes you really h<u>o</u>:t and
     really th<u>i</u>rsty—
  9. Julie: Eu::w!
 10. Crystal: Heh. Yeah. huh huh
 11. Julie: That sounds awful!

In her description in [7] of what it was like to take Ecstasy, Crystal likens the drug to *really mild acid*. She then elaborates on this statement, saying *That's what it made me feel, y'know just the colors an' the y'know uh the way it makes you think an' stuff.* Crystal appears to assume that Julie has taken acid before, and that based on this knowledge she will be able to infer what Ecstasy is like. In fact, Julie has never tried acid. Despite this fact, she demonstrates an understanding of Crystal's description in turn 5 with *Oh, is that what it is?*, as well as in turn 7, with *Mmhm*. Why would Julie indicate that she understands Crystal's comparison, without having tried either of the drugs being compared? It may be that she feels she has a kind of second-hand understanding of what it's like to take acid, just from hearing so many descriptions of it. She is also being invited (by *y'know* and *an' stuff*) to act as if she is familiar with what is being described.

Whether or not Julie actually shares the knowledge assumed by the speaker is not of any consequence. It is the *assumption* of shared knowledge that is marked by the general extender, not the fact, and that assumption is rarely challenged. Indeed, questioning an utterance containing a general extender might be perceived as a breach of the reciprocity of perspectives (the assumption that the hearer will supply whatever unstated understandings are required to make sense of the speaker's utterance). Rather than affirming the participants' similarity, this would draw attention to their differences and potentially increase the social distance between them.

Co-occurrence with *you know*

As markers of intersubjectivity, general extenders frequently co-occur with another expression that is often used to indicate assumed similarity of participants' experience: the discourse marker *you know*. In addition to occurring in many of the excerpts already cited, notably in examples [5], [6], and [7], the close co-occurrence of *y'know* with a general extender is highlighted in extracts [8]–[10].

[8]   (Roger and Sara are discussing how she might take over his apartment when he moves out)
  1. Roger: I will um intimate to the people who:: rent me this place
  2. Sara: Uh huh
  3. Roger: that there is someone who will y'know=like (.) take it over, and under my recommendation as **y'know— all that crap**, .hhhh // an' um
  4. Sara: Yeah.
  5. Roger: an' they will um—(.5) an' see—an' like see if I get any feedback on their intentions about what they wanna do.

[9]   (Maya is talking to Sara about a mutual friend who is about to marry and move to another state, and her desire to keep in touch with that friend)

1. Maya: I mean I don't approve of what she's doing (.5)
   but (1.5) I'd really like to like if she's gonna go
   through labor and delivery and she's gonna have a
   baby **and all this stuff** (.5) **you know** I'd // like to be
   able to be there.
2. Sara: I—I—I think she—I think she'll keep in touch
   with you.

[10]   (Crystal is telling Julie about her surprise in finding
        Julie's wedding announcement in her mailbox)
1. Crystal: For some reason I just looked in the mailbox, I
   didn't even think there'd be:: anything, y'know'
2. Julie: Uh huh
3. Crystal: I just was gonna take garbage out of it **or**
   s(h)omething, y'(h)know, huh huh I didn't know
   what was in there! huh huh . . .

The co-occurrence of *you know* with general extenders is not limited to
my data set. The following excerpts, [11]–[13], are from other data
sources, representing different interactive situations, but they demonstrate the same phenomenon.

[11] Ken: I go in there and I uh put all the bottles in back
     and I uh give people change, **and junk like this.** // **Y'know.**
     Roger: Last Saturday night I downed a litre bottle of
     champagne . . . (Jefferson 1990: 70)

[12] (An elderly man is talking about his youth)
     There were + some very very good houses rather old—
     fashioned but quite good houses + with very big rooms and
     that + and these were sort of better class people + people
     with maybe + minor civil servants **and things like that you**
     know that had been able to afford + dearer rents **and that**
     in those days **you know** ++ but the average working-class
     man + the wages were very small + the rents would run
     from anything from about five shillings to + seven shillings
     which was about all they could've possibly afforded in
     those days . . . (Brown and Yule 1983b: 17)

[13] He just kept talking about life being a game **and all.**
     You know. (Salinger 1945: 12)

The fact that general extenders and the discourse marker *you know*
frequently co-occur seems to support the notion that, in using a general

extender, a speaker is relying on an assumption of shared knowledge or experience (see Aijmer 1985: 378–379; Overstreet and Yule 1997b). According to Schiffrin, one function of *you know* is to mark "general consensual truths which speakers assume their hearers share through their co-membership in the same culture, society, or group" (1987: 274). *You know* may also be used to seek interactional alignments by establishing shared opinion (Schiffrin 1987). In such cases, a hearer may affirm his or her shared knowledge or perspective with utterances such as *yeah, umhm, uh huh, okay,* or *right.*

Backchannels

Like the discourse marker *you know,* general extenders may also elicit displays of understanding. In such cases, hearers often indicate their shared knowledge with backchannels, as illustrated in [14]–[16].

[14] 1. Sara: the first (.) order of importance is to find a
place to li::ve.
2. Roger: Right. (.) Ah, yeah. We've made a list of you—
for you of like doctors a::nd connections, **an' thi//ngs**
3. Sara: Yea:::h.
4. Roger: Yea::h You'll find a place to live, and you'll find
a job. Don't worry about that.
5. Sara: Oh, no. I'm not worried about that at all.

[15] 1. Anne: Wull that's the way—that's who I was until
2. Roger: Uh huh
3. Anne: I got a PhD **or something**=
4. Roger: =Oh, okay. Right.
5. Anne: So it was u::m=
6. Roger: =Yeah, I—I know what you mean. Yeah.

[16] 1. Maya: looking at my grandma and my grandpa: I—
they're not freaked out about dying even (.) my
grandmother who doesn't have religion is (.5) you know
I mean they have like little (.) bizarre times in their
lives where they're like kinda shaky and I think
that's dealing with it but (.) they seem to have a much
better grip on the fact (.) that they're gonna die and
much more at peace with it regardless of (.) affiliations
or like intelligence **or any//thing**.
2. Sara: Mmhm.
3. Maya: I'm sure it's all (.) real biological but (.) hnh! . . .

Again, this phenomenon is not limited to my data set. For example, Dines notes that her data contained no instances of requests for clarification by hearers; instead, there was "supportive feedback indicating that they were following the communication" (1980: 30). The following are illustrations from other data sources:

[17] B: and you'll find you see you've always got some
　　　research to do you can // always get on with some
　　　A: (Yes)
　　　B: slips **or something** // so you'll never
　　　A: m
　　　B: be in that happy position (laughs)
　　　(Svartvik and Quirk 1980: 133)

[18] B: or then they (he found) last year that that five fifteen
　　　one clashed with they some of them had phonetics **or**
　　　something
　　　A/C: (mhm)
　　　B: and he said well what about half past seven
　　　(Svartvik and Quirk 1980: 128)

[19] K: . . . there were twelve I put in there and they were just
　　　over twelve pound each **or something**
　　　C: mmm　(Cheepen and Monaghan 1990: 121)

[20] I: . . . so it's not it's not to do with building it's to do with
　　　who owns . the bit of ground . under the building it was very
　　　much property law . **that kind of thing**
　　　G: mm　(Cheepen and Monaghan (1990: 121)

As part of her analysis of *y'know*, Schiffrin claims that once we acknowledge that the information state is verbally displayed (as it is in the examples above) "we may also assume that the marker by which such verbal displays are SOLICITED functions not merely as a cognitive marker, but as an interactional marker" (1987: 273). In accordance with this description, general extenders can also be considered interactional markers. It is important to emphasize this interactive or interpersonal function served by general extenders, if only to dispel the pervasive notion that they can be serving only the type of referential function assumed in studies of categorization. Whether or not they can be used on occasion as category implicative devices in shared referential worlds, they are certainly used with greater frequency as interactional markers of intersubjectivity in shared social worlds.

Having established that general extenders serve a major interactive function, it becomes possible to look at some of the more specific modal functions associated with their use on particular occasions. In the following chapters, I will explore some uses of general extenders to mark attitude toward the message or orientation to sociocultural norms.

–6–

Expectations, Evaluations, and Emphasis

Words like these are commonly described as sentence-adverbs.
Looked at from a semantic point of view, they can generally be seen
as having some kind of evaluative function. They are used by the
speaker in order to express, parenthetically, his opinion or
attitude towards the proposition that the sentence expresses or the
situation that the proposition describes.

Lyons (1977: 451–452)

In this description, Lyons is actually discussing sentence-initial adverbs such as *Frankly*, but in many respects, it is a remarkably accurate account of how some general extenders are used. Just as the sentence-initial adverbs in Lyons's analysis are used to express modality—the speaker's attitude to the proposition or situation described—so too are many of the general extenders that occur in interactive discourse.

In the previous chapter, the discussion shifted from a consideration of the potential ideational function of general extenders to an exploration of the interpersonal function of these forms. In this chapter, I will explore further the interpersonal function of general extenders; I will look at how certain expressions (*and everything, and all (that), or anything, or what*) may be used by speakers to mark an attitude toward a message expressed. In particular, following observations by other investigators (e.g., Aijmer 1985, Ward and Birner 1993), I will consider the ways in which speakers use general extenders as intensifiers, to emphasize or highlight a previous part of an utterance. We will see that, in using general extenders as intensifiers, speakers often express their evaluation of something as surprising or extreme. Such evaluations rely on an assumption that the speaker and hearer share an intersubjective concept of what is typical, normal, or expected in a given socio-cultural context.

The Unexpected

As Aijmer (1985) has noted, the forms *and everything* and *or anything* are often used by speakers to mark an attitude of surprise or astonishment toward an expressed message. The most obvious difference between the uses of these two general extenders is that *and everything* occurs in positive environments, whereas *or anything* occurs in negative environments. Both forms are used by the same speaker in the interaction presented in [1]. In this excerpt, Crystal is telling Julie about her struggle to get child support from her exhusband.

[1] 1. Crystal: He doesn't even know where (.) my new address—where to ch—send money to me y'kno//w **or anything**
   2. Julie: Oh, wo:::w
   3. Crystal: I kno::w, so I have to wait for it at my old address—Meanwhile I've already had to pay re:nt, an' so it's like he's just like expecting me to have this money::: y'know // like
   4. Julie: Mmhm
   5. Crystal: to just c—come up with, like no problem—
   6. Julie: Um//hm
   7. Crystal: It's unbelievable!
   8. Julie: Bummer.=
   9. Crystal: =Su:ch a jerk. So I'm just gonna—I'm getting a lawyer an' I'm just gonna y'know they're gonna send a messenger to Australia or have one over there just serve him papers (.) t//o his face
   10. Julie: Goo:d.
   11. Crystal: He's gonna hafta fly back special.
   12. Julie: heh heh heh // heh
   13. Crystal: Yeah. I'm gonna rea:::m him for // this one.
   14. Julie: huh huh huh huh huh huh // .hhh
   15. Crystal: He's making me so mad=I just found out he ripped me off **an' everything**
   16. Julie: He di:::d?
   17. Crystal: He's been sending me um, it's supposed to be three hundred dollars, but he's been deducting seventy dollars for insurance . . .

The first point of interest in excerpt [1] is in turn 1, where Crystal says *He doesn't even know where (.) my new address—where to ch—send money to me y'know or anything*. It appears that, in using the general extender *or anything*, Crystal marks the assertion that her ex-husband doesn't even know where to send money to her as astonishing, or difficult to believe. The adverb *even* in this utterance strengthens this implication by providing the conventional implicature "contrary to expectation." Note that in turn 2, Julie responds *Oh, wo:::w;* (although it is not clear in the transcript, the utterance of *wo:::w* occurs immediately after *or anything*). This expression of surprise may be seen as an empathetic response to Crystal's *or anything*. In turn 7, Crystal explicitly calls her ex-husband's behavior *unbelievable!*

A second point of interest in [1] is in turn 15, where Crystal says *I just found out he ripped me off an' everything*. In this case, Crystal's use of *and everything* seems to mark *he ripped me off* as unexpected and shocking behavior. Once again, Julie's response in turn 16 (*He di:::d?*) may be seen as a sympathetic response to this expression of outrage. The co-occurrence of one speaker's emotional expression via the general extender and the other speaker's shocked response provides a kind of interactive evidence for the functions of these general extenders, as the participants perceive them.

Further illustration of these points can be found in excerpt [2]. Here Maya is telling Sara about a recent interaction she had with their mutual friend named Wendy. In her initial summary of the events (turn 1), Maya simply reports what Wendy did, without including a general extender. However, in her dramatic re-enactment of the interaction (turn 3), she presents the same event, expressing it as a first person account and including the general extender *and everything*.

[2] 1. Maya: I don't know why: I always have arguments
          with Wendy=well, not re̲ally arguments. I—I call her
          (.) and I'm not perfectly happy with her and I'm not
          even yelling=and I'm not even a̲rguing. I'm just like
          "Okay, that's fine. I—I misunderstood you and you said
          you were gonna do this (.5) and I'm a little angry but
          that's okay and I'm gonna be over it in a minute" and I
          me̲a̲n it. "A—I—uh okay, I'm a little peeved but I'll
          get over it."=An' five minutes later I've forgotten it.
          Wendy goes into the bathroom—gets so scared sh//e
          takes a shi::t
     2. Sara: ((burps))
     3. Maya: .hhh! and then dr(h)ives to my house because
          she thinks she's in major trouble. I'm like (.5) "Me not

liking everything you do doesn't mea:n (.) that (.) I'm
m<u>a</u>d at you." You know, it's like (.) she comes over an'
she's like "I—I ran over here" an' I'm like "Why?
Why did—" Ø "I'm not gonna go with Sara because .hh
you're upset with—." I'm like "N<u>o</u>, I'm n<u>o</u>t upset with
you. I'm over it.=I'm completely over it.=I said 'That
pisses me off', and that got me over it." An'=she's like
(.5) "Oh, (.5) I took a shit **and everything** 'cause I was
so scared." heh heh Ø "Wo//w, a crapper."

4. Sara: Yea:h
5. Maya: I—I just um sh<u>a</u>ke when I get nervous. I don't go
   and empty anything unl<u>e::</u>ss I'm in a house that's being
   broken into an' then
6. Sara: huh=an' then I—//lose <u>a:</u>ll bowel control
7. Maya: all hell breaks loose. huh huh Yeah.

Excerpt [2] provides an especially interesting example of *and everything* functioning to mark a previous part of an utterance as surprising.
What makes this example particularly revealing is the fact that
Maya, in representing both sides of the reported conversation,
provides a response to her own utterance (represented as Wendy's
speech) which contains *and everything*. In turn 3, Maya reports that
Wendy said *I took a shit and everything 'cause I was so scared;* Maya
then reports her own reaction to this as *Wow, a crapper!* (Note that
the shift in speakers that occurs with *Wow* is marked in the transcript by the zero quotative symbol (Ø) which precedes it; see Mathis
and Yule 1994). The response of *wow* can again be seen as a reaction to
an utterance containing *and everything* which marks *I took a shit* as
surprising behavior. Since Maya's response (*wow*) displays an interpretation of her own utterance (*I took a shit and everything*), it seems
reasonable to assume that this interpretation of the utterance (i.e.,
surprising) matches its intended meaning.

Another clear example of *and everything* functioning to mark a
previous part of an utterance as surprising is offered in excerpt [3].

[3] Sally: Did you do Mardi Gras? Can you believe it's on the
     internet? King Cake and beads **and everything**! It was
     wild! (E-mail message, 2 Feb. 1996)

Here, Sally's use of *and everything* signals and reinforces her expression of surprise at something unexpected: that *Mardi Gras*, complete
with *King Cake and beads*, is on the Internet. Her surprise (and an
assumption that it will be shared) is also communicated via the
exclamation point and the phrase *Can you believe. . . ?*

In marking some information as unexpected, speakers sometimes use the form *or nothing (like that)* rather than *or anything*. A striking example of this form being used to mark something as surprising, or hard to believe, is presented in excerpt [4], from a novel written in a Scottish dialect, in which *nowt* represents *nothing*.

[4]   John Deaf's hoose wis weird. Ah mean, thir wis eywis some
        scruffy hooses in the scheme, bit nowt like John Deaf's. Fir
        a start, John Deaf's hoose hud fuck all in it; nae furniture **or
        nowt like that.** Nowt oan the flair, no even any lino. Jist
        they cauld black tiles thit ivray hoose hud, fir the
        underflair heatin thit nae cunt could afford tae switch oan.
        (Welsh 1994: 99)

This description of John Deaf's house begins with the observation that it was *weird* and unlike any others. Following this is an example of how it was weird (and thus surprising): the house had *nae furniture or nowt like that*.

Or nothing is also used to highlight something extraordinary (and thus surprising) in the cartoon caption in figure 6.1. In this case, the surprising element is stated in the first phrase *That was incredible*, and the negative general extender is attached to the end of a set of four (surprisingly) non-present features. Unlike other creatures these alligators normally eat, the ones they just devoured didn't have any of the expected drawbacks such as *fur, claws, horns*, or *antlers!*

The Most and Least Expected

Having suggested that certain general extenders are used with a "contrary to expectation" assumption, I can now focus more precisely on their distinct functions. One way to look at the different functions of the forms *and everything/and all* versus *or anything/or nothing* is to view the former as indicating a maximum extreme, and the latter as indicating a minimum extreme. Under such an analysis, the maximum might represent the *most*, and the minimum might represent the *least* that would be expected in a given situation. For example, in excerpt [3], the general extender *and everything* may mark the inclusion of *King Cake* and *beads* in the Internet's Mardi Gras celebration as being at the far end (i.e., the maximum) of what one might expect to find in conjunction with a Mardi Gras celebration. In excerpt [4], the general extender *or nowt like that* marks (some) *furniture* as something one would (minimally) expect to find in a person's house.

THE FAR SIDE   By GARY LARSON

"That was incredible. No fur, claws, horns, antlers, or nothin'... Just soft and pink."

Figure 6.1. Alligators. The Far Side © 1983 Farworks, Inc.
Used by permission of Universal Press Syndicate. All rights reserved.

Excerpts [5]–[8] are further examples of *and everything* used to mark some kind of maximum extreme. In excerpt [5], Blake and Donna are making plans to get a new kitten.

[5] 1. Donna: So: um (.) um—um—um—um, Thursday morning.
     2. Blake: Yes.
     3. Donna: I'd say at least ten o'clock, we should meet, 'cause (.) I don't wanna um:::: c—waste too much time—I mean I don't want it to be like // (too)
     4. Blake: Do you have the cat picked out **and everything**?
     5. Donna: Yeah. It—we're—it's the: cat we're picking up. I mean, this one particular cat.

In turn 3, Donna expresses a desire not to *waste too much time*. In response to this, Blake asks Donna *Do you have the cat picked out and everything?* Here, *and everything* may be seen to mark *you have the cat picked out* as the maximum that Donna could have done to ensure that the task of picking up the kitten would not take too much time.

Examples of *and everything* used to mark a maximal extreme are also found in excerpts [6]–[8], from other sources.

[6]   The President's new Labrador pup got to go with the family on vacation last week, riding in style on Air Force One **and everything**. (*Honolulu Advertiser*, 28 June 1998)

[7]   I'm back—only it's worse than I thought. They're not only sticking us for ga::s, but they're grabbing tires **and E:verything**! They're really socking it to us. (*The Jerk*, a film)

[8]   I knew I would leave you with babies **and everything**. (*The Cure*, "Disintegration")

In excerpt [6], from a newspaper article about President Clinton's pets, the writer uses *and everything* to mark *riding on Air Force One* as an extreme privilege to be granted to a canine. In excerpt [7], from a film, the character played by Steve Martin is on the telephone with the police. As he tries to report the extreme seriousness of a crime in progress, he reports that the thieves are not only taking *ga::s, but they're grabbing tires, and everything!* The general extender *and everything* is used to mark the taking of *tires* as extreme (and thus surprising) behavior. Finally, in excerpt [8], from a popular song, an angst-ridden male sings of the inevitable disintegration of love relationships, and the soul-disintegrating pain that follows. He says to his lover that he knew he would leave her *with babies and everything*. In this example, the break-up that leaves another *with babies* is marked as extremely painful and an extreme example of the disintegration of a relationship.

The form *and all* may also function to mark a maximum extreme, or the most that would be expected in a given situation. Consider excerpt [9], from an advertisement for weedkiller.

[9]   Kills even tough weeds roots **and all**. (*Honolulu Advertiser*, 23 Aug. 1998)

Here, the general extender *and all* seems to mark the claim that the product kills the *roots*, as well as the rest of the plant, as an extreme, or the most which could be expected. In [10], from an article about quarterback Brett Favre, the writer emphasizes that the acceptance of Wisconsin's *cold* is the most extreme form of acceptance possible.

[10] The Super Bowl champ and two-time NFL MVP seems to
      have adopted Wisconsin, cold **and all**. (*USA Weekend,*
      21–23 March 1997)

In contrast to these maximum-extreme uses of general extenders, we also have minimum-extreme uses. Excerpts [11]–[13] illustrate the use of *or anything* to indicate a minimum extreme, or the least that would be expected in a given socio-cultural context. Excerpt [11] is taken from a conversation in a hospital emergency room. Karen and Donna, part of the medical staff, are discussing a patient who recently died there without any friends or family at his side.

[11] 1. Donna: He didn't look familiar, but I mean in his
             condition::, hhh.
      2. Karen: No. He was a nice—he // was a nice—patient
      3. Donna: I 'member I had a nice memory about him
             though.
      4. Karen: Yeah. He was—he was really ni::ce. He
             was//n't uh
      5. Donna: I felt so sa::d for hi::m, an' no fami//ly
      6. Karen: Yea:h
      7. Donna: **or anythi::ng**, y//ea:h?
      8. Karen: Yeah.
      9. Donna: So sa::d. . . .

When an individual is sick and dying in the hospital, it might be said that there is an expectation that at least the family members of the patient (provided there are some) will come to be with him. In turns 5 and 7, Donna says *I felt so sad for him, an' no family or anything, yeah?* Donna's use of *or anything* in this example may be seen to mark the expectation that family would be present as minimal. The sadness she feels at this person's death is made more extreme by the fact that the person was alone. Note that in this example, there is lengthening of the vowel *i* in *anything*, which may play a role in designating the function of this form. I will return to the role of phonological marking at the end of this chapter.

The attendance of family at a significant event in one's life is also marked as minimally expected in the next example. In excerpt [12], Julie is telling Crystal about her recent marriage. Rather than planning a big wedding, Julie and her husband decided to get married in a small civil ceremony at the courthouse.

[12]   Crystal: So, but—your parents weren't there **or anything**?

Crystal's use of *or anything* appears to mark the attendance of Julie's parents at the wedding as something that would be minimally expected, and perhaps surprising if it did not occur.

A final example of *or anything* used to mark something as minimally expected is found in excerpt [13], from the play *Who's Afraid of Virginia Woolf?*

[13]   Martha: I don't know what you're so tired about . . . you
          haven't *done* anything all day; you didn't have any
          classes, **or anything.**   (Albee 1962: 7)

In this scene, George (a professor) and Martha (his wife), have just returned home from a party. It's 2:00 a.m., and Martha is in full swing. She wants to engage George in conversation, but George says he's too tired. Martha chides George, saying he has no reason to be tired; he *didn't have any classes, or anything.* In this case, having classes is the minimum Martha expects George to have done to justify being tired. This last example, dating from a representation of educated talk almost forty years ago, supports a view that the form and function of this general extender are neither new nor used exclusively by the young and uneducated.

Disclaiming Expected Interpretations

The two general extenders *or anything* and *and everything* that have been the focus of the preceding discussion can be found in two constructions that appear to have become almost formulaic in contemporary American English. Both constructions seem to be used to clarify the speaker's intention by drawing attention to an anticipated interpretation of some aspect of the speaker's behavior, and then disclaiming it.

One construction is of the type '*not* X *or anything, but* Y,' which can be illustrated in this (reconstructed) comment to a waiter: *I don't want to make a fuss or anything, but I ordered a salad.* The inclusion of *or anything* in this type of formulaic construction seems to indicate that a negative interpretation of the speaker's intention is possible but is being disclaimed. A disclaimer is recognized in studies of interactional sociolinguistics as an attempt to render potentially problematic actions (those that may be perceived as extraordinary or inexplicable) meaningful, and to define such actions as irrelevant for reassessment of the speaker's established identity (Hewitt and Stokes 1975; Bell, Zahn, and Hopper 1984). Disclaimers have been classified as a form of alignment talk (Goffman 1959), which has the general goal of sustaining joint social action. Unlike other forms of

alignment talk, which function retrospectively to mediate potentially problematic action, disclaimers are normally employed prior
to potentially problematic actions as a way of averting anticipated
trouble; for this reason they have also been called "preventatives"
(Goffman 1959, McLaughlin 1984).[1]

The other formulaic construction 'X *and everything, but* Y' can
be illustrated in this (reconstructed) comment from a woman about a
suitor: *I mean, he's really rich and everything, but I can't go out with
him*. The inclusion of *and everything* in this type of formulaic
construction emphasizes that the phenomenon expressed in X is the
case, yet it is not to be used as the basis of interpreting how the
speaker thinks or behaves, as presented in Y.

Both of these types of formulaic construction exhibit features of
what Baker (1975: 37) has called "response-controlling *but*-prefaces,"
and the kinds of response that the speaker is attempting to control
seem to involve possible evaluations of the speaker or "impression
management" (Goffman 1959: 208). A more detailed analysis of
general extenders within formulaic disclaimers is presented in
Overstreet and Yule (1999b).

Not X or anything, but Y

The formulaic construction *not X or anything, but* Y is conventionally
used to emphasize that a (perhaps extreme) behavior or intention is
NOT the case. The typical interpretation invited for this formula
appears to be: Y (doing or being something) could count as X (doing or
being something else), and I announce that it's not, before I proceed.
This pattern is present and highlighted in examples [14]–[16]. In
excerpt [14], Anne is describing the transcendental experience she had
on a recent trip to another country.

[14]   (Anne is telling Roger about her recent trip to Ireland)
  1. Anne: I wanna get back to Ireland. I really hhh. um:
  2. Roger: Need it? (1.0)
  3. Anne: Yeah, I was g—uh o:h that—some (.) y'know—
      some ni:ght I'll—if I c'n still remember um (.) I'll tell
      you some of the stuff that happened (.) // there
  4. Roger: Uh huh
  5. Anne: It's just spending time alo::ne, like I really—
      I traveled all over the country but I did it by myself
      // I just
  6. Roger: Right
  7. Anne: y'know (.) and um (.) n̲o̲t to try to get too mystical
      or anything, but a lot of the s—I didn't—I:: didn't ta̲:lk
      to anybody, // huh huh huh

8. Roger: Uh huh
9. Anne: b—but a lot of the stuff was just (.) It's a long time since I've (.5) had a lot of experiences at a sort of non-verbal non-neocortex level . . .

Perceiving that this kind of talk might seem extreme, or at least not typical or expected among competent members of their socio-cultural group, Anne attempts to manage Roger's impression of her by acknowledging how she might sound to him (*too mystical*). In doing so, she defines her behavior as an irrelevant basis for a re-evaluation of her identity (as incompetent, or as having lost control of herself or her mind). A second example, with a similar function, is found in excerpt [15], from Tsui's data.

[15] P: I mean I I mean I I y'know it's it's a problem I mean they asked me oh something about do you give blood. I said well I'm not allowed to give blood. Why not? Well I had malaria and I can never give blood. How did you get malaria? Well I was in the jungles in Zambia. Y'know, and and it's not that I'm boasting **or anything** but I =
S: [You're not.
P: = have done certain things in my life and they asked about it.   (1994: 151)

Faced with the potential problematic action of presenting herself in a socially dispreferred way (i.e., *me better than you*) that might cause the hearer to view her negatively, the speaker interrupts her story with a formulaic disclaimer. Interestingly, in this example the hearer provides supportive feedback immediately after the *not X or anything*, but before the *but Y* part. This supportive interlocutor indicates that regardless of what the speaker is about to say, no negative evaluation of her will occur. Now consider excerpt [16], from a newspaper article quoting Reggie Miller, the U.S. Olympic Basketball Team's "biggest trash talker" on the eve of a game in Toronto.

[16] We don't want to cause any international incidents **or anything**, but we'll get angrier in Toronto.   (*Honolulu Star Bulletin*, 1 Aug. 1994)

This example was widely quoted in the sports media just before the U.S. team was to play an international match in preparation for the Olympics. In producing this utterance, Miller acknowledges a potentially problematic action (anger and loss of control), but he uses it to deny certain intentions (causing international incidents). Interestingly, in this case, the intentions being denied are set at such an improbable level that the formula seems to highlight the potentially problematic action rather than to disclaim it.[2]

Because the first part of the pattern *not X or anything* has become established formulaically as a way of clarifying intention, it can be so used without the second part of the formula (*but* Y) being articulated. In examples [17]–[19], the speakers use the first part of the pattern to mark an attempt to clarify an intention. In [17], Rosie is telling Julie about her recent encounter with an attractive young guy.

[17] 1. Rosie: I think that I've pretty much set him in his
              place, I mean in a nice way but I—you know, I mean, I'm
              married, so I have no intention of—I don't even know
              him and I think we have a long ways to go before
              there's ever even an issue=That's not even a—a—pa—
              potentia::l for anything else—any more than being
              friends right now.
       2. Julie: Uh huh
       3. Rosie: Because we don't even know each other. So::
              y'//know
       4. Julie: Okay
       5. Rosie: all that other woo-woo stuff is just um (.) that—
              just that. heh heh heh Kind of—kinda blew me away,
              but u::h it's ni::ce an' I just made it clear that we have
              to keep it really sweet an' y'know (.) really innocent.
              And um that's the way it is.
       6. Julie: Okay, Madam Wazel.
       7. Rosie: I'm not tryin' to fall in love **or anything**, that's
              for sure.
       8. Julie: heh heh heh heh // heh heh
       9. Rosie: Shit! Let's complicate your life!

Because she is separated from her husband but not yet divorced, Rosie feels that it is inappropriate to fall in love with someone else. She uses the formula *not X or anything* to clarify her intentions, where *X* = *trying to fall in love*.

In excerpt [18], Maya is reporting on a previous interaction between her friend Tracy and Tracy's boyfriend. Tracy's boyfriend had *fucked someone else*, which had upset Tracy. The speaker (Maya) presents a more extreme and negative interpretation of the boyfriend's behavior, before disclaiming it.

[18] Maya: So he ca:lled like two hours later an' she was in
              bed an' she woke up an' um (.) he was like "Tracy, Tracy"
              and she was like "What? What happened? Wha—what

happened? Is something wrong?"=And he wouldn't talk
and she said "You fucked someone else" and he started
crying—He's like (.) "I'm sorry—I just blah blah blah
blah" an' she's like "I can't believe—How could you do
this to me? How the fuck could you do—" and just cursed at
him=hung up the phone=he came home (.) an' he was so
upset an' so freaked out by it and had told her
immediately after it had happened and like obviously
felt real bad and wasn't tryin' to like (.) y'know see
someone on the side **or anything.**=He just fucked up and felt
ba:d.

According to the report, although Tracy's boyfriend had sex with
someone else, he felt bad about it, and did not intend to see the other
person regularly: (he) *wasn't tryin' to like (.) y'know see someone on
the side or anything*. The speaker is claiming that the boyfriend's
behavior should be treated as a mistake rather than as the basis for a
negative retypification.

Finally, in excerpt [19], Sara wants to know how much of Roger's
stuff she can buy (or have) when she takes over his apartment.

[19] 1. Sara: So but like later on, I'm gonna get together with
              you an' find out like how much of your stuff you wanna
              get rid of, an' how much of it you wanna sell to me, heh!
     2. Roger: O:::kay.
     3. Sara: Like are you—I me—Are you like (.) planning to
              do that? I mean, I don't wanna step on your toes **or
              anything.**

Realizing that she is in danger of imposing on the hearer and thereby
violating a rule of politeness, Sara, in the final line of [21], disavows
that intention with the *not X or anything* part of a formulaic
disclaimer. Including an idiom (*don't wanna step on your toes*) that
would represent extreme imposition if taken literally, Sara expresses
only the first part of the disclaimer as a negative politeness strategy.
I will consider politeness aspects of general extenders in more detail
in chapter 7.

X and everything, but Y

The general extender *and everything* is also used in a formulaic
construction: X *and everything, but* Y. The typical interpretation for
this construction appears to be, "I acknowledge X, but nevertheless
assert Y." Often, Y represents the speaker's intention. Consider the
following excerpt from an interview with actor Tom Cruise.

[20] Cruise: I was a wild kid. I'd cut school **and everything**, but
      it really had to do with my wanting always to push the
      envelope to see, Where do I stand with myself?
      (Sessums 1994: 195, 270)

While Cruise acknowledges that he cut school (a potentially extreme
form of nonconformity consistent with that of *a wild kid*), he asserts
that his behavior was a reflection of a noble intention—it had to do
with wanting to test himself and grow as an individual.

A second example of this is found in excerpt [21].

[21] K: + I mean we + know he's a crabby old sod and he's a
      miserable bugger **and everything** . but better the devil you
      know (laughing) than the one you don't . . .
      (Cheepen and Monaghan 1990: 155)

In the preceding discussion, K had expressed concern that a new
teacher might turn out to be a disappointment. Here, K acknowledges
that the old teacher has extremely negative characteristics (*he's a
crabby old sod and he's a miserable bugger and everything*), but she
would nevertheless like to see him stay (*better the devil you know
than the one you don't*).

The forms *and all (that)* and *and all the rest of it* also occur in
this construction. In [22], Maya is talking about Wendy, who doesn't
take good care of her pets.

[22] Maya: And I mean (.) she is the—the caretaker of the dog
      and all that but I—I'm real serious about it. If she gets a
      pe:t in the next few years I'm gonna slap her.

In this example, Maya acknowledges Wendy's rights as the caretaker
of the dog (which she had put to sleep), but she nevertheless asserts
her intention to slap Wendy if she gets another pet anytime soon.

In [23], from a newspaper report, a gay Episcopalian priest is
talking about the death threats he has been receiving in the mail
from those who oppose his lifestyle.

[23] It's the usual stuff, "scourge of God," "crime against nature"
      and all that, but recently a friend from San Diego called
      and suggested I should watch my packages and lock the car.
      (*Honolulu Star Bulletin*, 24 Feb. 1996)

The priest acknowledges that the mail he has been receiving represented attacks of a particular kind and was not unusual, but he nevertheless expresses concern that attacks against him may escalate into
something more serious.

An example from written language is presented in excerpt [24].

[24] I kept thinking I had to try and look indifferent, which
      was weird, because on some level I *am* indifferent to him.
      I mean, he's cute and he's powerful **and all that**, but you
      have to take his reputation into account. He's a former
      cocaine addict and he fucks *whores*. (Fisher 1987: 119)

In [24], the narrator is talking about a guy she has been dating. She
acknowledges that he's cute and he's powerful (qualities normally
given positive value), but she nevertheless asserts that, because of
his bad reputation, she's indifferent to him.

One co-occurrence feature present in many of these extracts is
worth noting. In extracts [17], [19], [21], [22], and [24], the part of the
utterance preceding the general extender is prefaced by the discourse
marker *I mean*. According to Schiffrin, *I mean* occurs in explanations of
intention, particularly when the speaker suspects that the intended
force of a previous utterance is "too indirect for appropriate uptake"
(1987: 296). It should not be surprising that *I mean* is found in co-occurrence with a general extender formula used to clarify the speaker's
intention, particularly when some type of "contrary to expectation"
message is involved.

Is this an Intensifier, *or what*?

The addition of *or anything* and *and everything* to a message often
provides an emphatic or intensifying effect. Another general extender
that can function as an intensifier is *or what*. Consider the following
examples.

[25]   (Julie's mother, Jean, has just received a funny
          picture of Julie's boyfriend in the mail).
      1. Julie: Is that the best picture **or what**?
      2. Jean: Sssh! It's absolutely priceless.

[26] 1. Donna: Do I have the cutest cat in the world **or what**?
      2. Blake: ((breathy voice)) I love your pussy.

In each of these examples, *or what* is appended to a yes/no question
that contains an evaluative assessment of some kind. This construction
can be represented as $X = Y$, *or what*? The interpretation invited for
this formula appears to be, "I think X, don't you agree?" By using this
construction, the speaker not only expresses an evaluation but also
solicits agreement from the hearer with his or her assessment that $X
= Y$. Indeed, in each of the above excerpts, the hearer overtly reponds

to the invited agreement with the speaker's assessment. In [25], Jean responds to Julie's *Is that the best picture or what?* with *Sssh! It's absolutely priceless*; in [26], Blake responds to Donna's *Do I have the cutest cat in the world or what?* with *I love your pussy*. The nature of the response helps us make sense of the function of the expression that elicited the response.

Excerpt [27] is an example of this structure from a written source. At the end of an article on gardening in which he proclaims the wonders of composting, the journalist concludes with what looks like a question. Without *or what*, this would be an odd question to ask. With *or what* marking the desired response as agreement, the function is clearly not really a yes/no question.

[27] Is this good stuff **or what**?
      (Honolulu Advertiser, 30 June 1996)

It is important to note that *or what* is used to solicit agreement with one's views, rather than a positive answer. For example, consider [28], said by a U.S. congressman criticizing a proposal made by President Clinton.

[28] Does he think we just got off a banana boat, **or what**?

Here, the congressman is not inviting a positive answer; he is soliciting agreement with his view that President Clinton is treating him and his fellow congressmen (and perhaps the broader public) as naïve and unsophisticated. He is soliciting agreement with what he thinks, not actually with what he just said.

As illustrated in examples [25]–[28], an assessment preceding the general extender *or what* typically pertains to third person entities. There are, however, occasional instances in which the speaker offers an evaluative assessment of herself (first person) or the hearer (second person), followed by *or what*. It is important to see self-assessments quite differently from the assessments of third person entities. In instances where the assessment is a negative one, agreement with the speaker may be neither appropriate nor expected. For example, consider excerpt [29], in which Donna is talking about her obsession with the actor Keanu Reeves.

[29] 1.   Donna: Am I psychotic **or what**?
     2.   Blake: Yes.
     3.   Donna: I mean if you—You kno:w me an' love me (.5)
     4.   Blake: ⌜ Correct.
     5.   Donna: ⌞ (*) So::: (.) you can: tolerate all this=but
          am I: (.5)
     6.   Blake: Psychotic! No, you're just a little boy crazy

In turn 1, Donna offers a negative evaluation of herself, followed by *or what*, in *Am I psychotic or what?* In turn 2, Blake responds to this with *Yes.* However, by responding in agreement with her negative self-evaluation, Blake is in danger of committing a face-threatening act. In fact, in turn 6, he withdraws his agreement, saying *No, you're just a little boy crazy*, indicating that he was just teasing Donna by going along with her negative self-evaluation. (See chapter 7 for further discussion of face and politeness.)

Another revealing example of how *or what* can be used is offered in [30], from a novel written in Hawaii Creole English. In this excerpt, the narrator (a teenage girl named Lovey) is reporting an interaction she had with her neighbor (Katy, a young woman pregnant with her first child and trying to decide on a name for the child).

[30] I give her my suggestions since lately I've been Katy's main
      visitor. "Autumn, Summer, or Heather for a girl." Katy
      winces. "What, what?" I tell her. Then she says nothing so
      I continue. "Christopher, Michael, or Dennis for a boy."
      Katy turns her eyebrows down. Katy says, "When the
      baby comes, I let you bathe him and change his diaper like
      that. But no name him—you too haolified with your names
      Lovey. Who you think you? Sometimes you act too haole-
      ish to me. You crazy—you like be haole **or what**?"
      (Yamanaka 1996: 45)

The point of interest in this excerpt is where Katy says *you like be haole or what?* In Katy's view, Lovey is acting like she wants to be a haole (originally a term for "newcomer" in Hawaiian, now often used for "white person"). And for this speaker, wanting to be a haole is clearly a negative thing. Rather than offering these haole names, Lovey should be coming up with more traditionally "local" names. It seems unlikely that Katy is seeking Lovey's agreement with her assessment of Lovey's behavior. Instead, it seems that Katy uses the general extender to mark her assessment of this behavior as surprising and to emphasize her surprise.

Where it does not follow evaluative assessments, *or what* may be used to urge an answer to a question (either direct or indirect). As demonstrated in [31] and [32], the emphasis added is clearly not about another choice, but about giving an answer.

[31] (83-year-old Scottish woman, holding a pot of tea over a
      cup and waiting to pour)
      Grandmother: Did you want it strong or weak **or what**?
      Grandson: Strong.

[32] (Husband and wife, discussing husband's gambling)
      Shirley: You never told me if you wo:n or lo:st **or wha:t.**
      Randy: I won.

In each of these instances, the hearer responds by providing an answer
to the question from the choices provided.

A Note on Phonological Prominence

When used as intensifiers, general extenders are used in their basic
form and typically do not contain the comparative elements *like this*
or *like that.* In addition, they are often accompanied by markers of
phonological prominence, such as loudness, vowel lengthening, and
rising pitch (cf. Ward and Birner 1993). This can be seen in the
transcriptions of some of the previous excerpts, including: [7], [11], [25],
[26], [29], and [32]. A particularly clear example is found in excerpt
[33], from a talk show. In this example, a male audience member is
telling a story about a time when he took his wife (then his fiancée)
out drinking, and she became ill.

[33] 1. Male: I put her in bed an' everything 'n took her clothes
          an' washed 'em while she was sleepin' there and I said
          I love you an' I respect you and I won't (.) d<u>o:</u> anything
      2. Audience: A:::::::::::://::hhhhh!
      3. Host: That is (1.0) He: washed her CL<u>O</u>:::::::thes **an'**
          <u>E</u>:verything! How long you been married?
      4. Male: Fourteen years.

In addition to exhibiting rising intonation, this instance of *and everything* is pronounced with heavy stress on the first syllable of *every.*
The speaker in this case is clearly not emphasizing "other things"
done by this man; she is focusing attention on the significance of the
action (*washed her clothes*). Indeed, it seems that any type of phonological prominence used with the general extenders *and everything,*
or anything, and *or what* serves to indicate that these expressions are
being used as intensifiers.

In this chapter, we have seen how general extenders can be used to
communicate an evaluation of something, based on an intersubjectively shared knowledge of what is typical, normal, or expected in a
given socio-cultural context. Having explored how speakers employ
some general extenders to mark attitude to message, I will next extend
the discussion of interpersonal function to consider the marking of
attitude to interlocutor.

–7–

Politeness

A: do you know. . . did you get anything back on those forms
ah . . . you had me fill out?
B: Hm . . . like what?
A: I wondered if they sent you a receipt or anything or a copy
of—
B: You mean your employment forms?
A: Yea.

Gumperz (1984: 284)

The fragment quoted here is from an interaction between a recently
appointed research assistant (A) and a secretary (B). In his analysis
of this brief interaction, Gumperz does not mention the use of the
general extender *or anything*, but he is clearly aware of its function in
creating the overall tone of A's talk: "Throughout the interaction, A
has pursued a strategy of not providing detailed information and
relying on B's ability to guess. Why he should do this is outside the
scope of this analysis" (1984: 285). One linguistic element in the strategy identified by Gumperz is the use of the general extender to try to
reduce the sense of imposition created by A's request. Explaining such
uses takes us into the study of politeness.

In this chapter, I will extend my analysis of the interpersonal
function of general extenders and investigate how a speaker's use of
these expressions can be viewed in terms of politeness. Specifically, I
will show how the use of an adjunctive general extender can function
as a strategy of positive politeness, and how the use of a disjunctive
general extender can function as a strategy of negative politeness.

Before doing so, however, it is helpful to review briefly what is generally understood by "politeness" as a technical term.

Politeness

The term "politeness," as used in the analysis of linguistic interaction, denotes a particular kind of behavior (see Brown and Levinson 1987). It is based on the concept that, as competent members of society, each of us has an image of self or "face" that we want to preserve, and that we want others to respect (Goffman 1967). There are two dimensions to face. Positive face can be defined as an individual's desire that her wants be desirable to others, and negative face is an individual's desire to do as she pleases without interference from others. We might say that positive face involves a need to be connected, and negative face involves a need to be independent. Although it is assumed that members of society generally cooperate and assume the cooperation of others in preserving face, interlocutors are nevertheless aware of the fact that face is always at risk (Goffman 1971). In order to minimize this risk, they employ politeness strategies.

Just as there are two types of face, there are two types of politeness strategies. Positive politeness strategies are those that are directed toward positive face and that mark solidarity. For example, one strategy of positive politeness is to use linguistic forms that indicate that the speaker and hearer belong to the same group and have certain things in common. Consider the following exchange between two graduate students.

[1]   Alice: Hey, where were you yesterday?
       Malia: I had an appointment with Eyebrows.

In this exchange, Malia uses the word *Eyebrows* to refer to a professor who doesn't speak much but, rather bizarrely, prefers to communicate by moving his eyebrows. In using an in-group expression known only to a small number of graduate students, Malia expresses a sense of solidarity with Alice and emphasizes an assumption of shared experiences, goals, and values.

Negative politeness strategies are those that are employed by speakers to minimize a threat to the hearer's negative face, to avoid imposing, and to mark deference. One way in which a speaker may threaten a hearer's negative face is by putting pressure on the hearer to do something. For instance, consider the following request I received from a friend.

[2] (Debbie had moved to another of the Hawaiian islands,
and I had been storing her vacuum cleaner for her in
Honolulu)
1. Debbie: I know you're busy, but would you deliver my
vacuum cleaner to the airport for me?
2. Mary: Uh, well, (.5) okay.

This rather unusual request is a good example of how a speaker might
impose on a hearer, by putting pressure on the hearer to do something.
In prefacing her request with *I know you're busy*, Debbie acknowledges that her request may threaten my negative face, and she indicates her sensitivity to this infringement on my freedom of action.
There are many conventional expressions in English (e.g., *I'm sorry to
bother you*, *Could I interrupt you for a second?*) that are commonly
used as part of a negative politeness strategy. More extended discussion of these issues can be found in Kasper (1994), R. Lakoff (1990),
Scollon and Scollon (1983), and Yule (1996). In the discussion that
follows, I will focus on the role played by general extenders in marking positive and negative politeness.

Invited Solidarity *an' stuff*

In chapter five, we noted that, in using a general extender, a speaker
invokes an assumption of intersubjectivity and communicates the
following message to the hearer: "Because we share the same knowledge, experience, and conceptual schemes, I do not need to be explicit;
you will be able to supply whatever unstated understandings are
required to make sense of my utterance." This is particularly true
when speakers use adjunctive general extenders, since the "more" that
is implicated is typically treated as known. Because one strategy of
positive politeness is to presuppose, raise, or assert common ground
with the hearer by demonstrating an assumption of shared knowledge
(Brown and Levinson 1987), the use of adjunctive general extenders can
generally be viewed as a strategy of positive politeness.

As we have seen in previous chapters, a wide variety of adjunctive general extenders can be used to mark an assumption of shared
knowledge. In this section, I will focus on the use of a particular form,
and stuff. In contemporary American English, this expression is
becoming one of the most common markers of connection or shared
experience. When used in this way, *and stuff* may not actually
intimate additional instances; instead, it may simply be used for the
purpose of marking invited solidarity as interactive partner, much
like the form *you know* (see Brown and Levinson 1987, Östman 1981,
Schiffrin 1987).

In excerpt [3], the full form *an' stuff like that* is used in a context where one speaker (Sara) is anticipating what she'll have to do when she moves to the city where her friend Roger lives.

[3] 1. Sara: an' the::n I'm gonna go do::wn (.) or I might go
            down to a temporary place an' like do a little testing
            .hhh a//n'
     2. Roger: Right.
     3. Sara: start sendin' out my resumé, **an' stuff like that,**
            but, I me//an,
     4. Roger: Right.
     5. Sara: the first (.) order of importance is to find a place
            to li::ve.
     6. Roger: Right. (.) Ah, yeah. We've made a list of you—
            for you of like doctors a::nd connections, an' thi//ngs
     7. Sara: Yea:::h.
     8. Roger: Yea::h. You'll find a place to live, and you'll
            find a job. Don't worry about that.

Throughout this part of the conversation, Sara has been talking about how she is going to cope with this big change in her life, and spelling out steps that she will have to take to get settled in a new city. In many ways, excerpt [3] is an appeal by Sara to Roger for confirmation that this will be a good way to go about getting a job. By completing her appeal with the general extender *an' stuff like that*, Sara is relying on Roger as someone whom she trusts to confirm for her that her plan is good. Indeed, Roger provides that confirmation, uttering *Right* several times before reassuring her that he will leave her *a list of doctors and connections and things*, and explicitly stating that everything will work out (*You'll find a place to live, and you'll find a job. Don't worry about that*). It is worth emphasizing that Sara's general extender (*an' stuff like that*) is not actually intimating other steps that Roger will be able to think of, but rather that Roger will generally provide supportive feedback and assure her that, given his experience in that context, she is right on track.

Excerpt [4] provides another example of a speaker using *and stuff* as an appeal to solidarity. Here, Bob and Pam are talking about a camping trip they are planning to take with their spouses and a few close friends. Bob had recently had brain surgery and was afraid it would be too difficult for him to hike the thirteen-mile trail to the campsite. Instead of hiking to the site, he was thinking about taking a boat along the coast and meeting the others there. In [4], Bob describes his problem, and concludes with an appeal to solidarity— *and stuff.*

[4] 1. Pam: Still having trouble with that (.5) equilibrium stuff?
     2. Bob: Wh—yeah. It—well—just walking.
     3. Pam: Mmhm
     4. Bob: Y'know uh if I pay attention I can do pretty good on flat surfaces but as soon as the .hhh surface gets uneven **an' stuff** um (.5) I—it—Yeah, it gets a little tricky.
     5. Pam Hmm. Bummer.

Bob is concerned that his inability to hike the trail might disrupt the group's plans. In using the general extender *an' stuff*, he appeals for understanding that hiking with poor equilibrium on an uneven trail can be tricky, and that his alternative plan is necessary. Pam provides a sympathetic reponse in line 5, with *Hmm. Bummer.*

Now consider excerpt [5]. In this excerpt, two friends are on a long-distance phone call. Sophie hates living in Los Angeles and is homesick for Hawai'i, where Lani lives and attends graduate school. Sophie is remarking on how pleasant the people at the University in Hawai'i are.

[5] 1. Sophie: 'Cause I talked to the grad division yesterday an' it's so weird, y'know, I call—I call the school **an' stuff** an everybody's so nice. It's just—It almost brings tears to my eyes to talk to someone an' not have full-on gatekeeper syndrome, y'know, an' .hhh // Just
     2. Lani: Mmhm.
     3. Sophie: to talk to somebody no::rmal .hhh y'know, an' you ask 'em a nice question politely, an' they're really nice to you:: or they try to he//lp you::
     4. Lani: Mmhm. Mmhm.=
     5. Sophie: =an' it's like I—I just can't—I'm blown away. Y'know it's like God, I—I—I almost forgot people are like this!
     6. Lani: Yeah.

The point of interest in this exchange is found in turn 1, where Sophie says *I call the school an' stuff.* It is unclear what, if any, additional instances might be implicated by the general extender *an' stuff.* Contextual constraints rule out the possibility that she might mean something like "drop by the school," since Sophie is in Los Angeles, and the university is in Hawai'i. It seems that Sophie's use of *an' stuff* invokes shared knowledge and experience of how great it is to live in Hawai'i, and that it represents an appeal for understanding of how hard it is for her to live in Los Angeles. Lani confirms her understanding with *Mmhm* in lines 2 and 4, and *Yeah* in line 6.

The use of *and stuff* as a marker of solidarity is even more transparent in excerpt [6], from data in Schiffrin (1994a: 212).

[6] IVer: Did you have older brothers and sisters **and stuff**?
     Gary: I have an older brother and a younger sister.
     Like we're all two years apart. So like my brother he's
     gonna be twenty six, and I'll be twenty-four in August.

The point of interest in [6] is where the interviewer (IVer) asks the question *Did you have older brothers and sisters and stuff?* It seems unlikely that, in using *and stuff*, the interviewer has additional instances in mind (i.e., *brothers, sisters, and ??*). Instead, the interviewer's use of *and stuff* is more like a punctuation feature than a form of reference.

It appears that, in British English, the form *and that* may perform a similar function. Consider the following examples from Macaulay.

[7] and he was flying fae Prestwick across to Ireland **and that**
     (i.e., to Ireland and nowhere else)

[8] but I remember him when he worked in the pits **and that**
     (i.e., when he worked in the pits and nowhere else)
     (1985: 113–114)

According to Macaulay (1985: 115), the function of *and that* in these excerpts is "clearly not set-marking." Instead, *and that* is used to appeal to a sense of shared knowledge and functions "as a kind of punctuation feature, almost the oral equivalent of a comma or a full stop, depending on intonation."

As exemplified in the following excerpt, the usage of *and stuff* as a kind of punctuation feature occurs quite frequently in the speech of some speakers. In [9], Crystal is telling Julie about her relationship with a younger guy.

[9] 1. Crystal: Frederico is just super—he's super mature for
         his age though, 'cause he's he sailed around the world
         s—um (.) for four yea::rs and (.) just sorta—an' had
         older brothers, y'kno::w, and come from a really
         wealthy family::=had a lot of experiences **and stuff**, so
         he really (1.0) kinda presents himself as being older.
     2. Julie: Umhm.
     3. Crystal: But he's a cool guy. We're just really taking it

slo:w 'cause he just got really really bu:rned **'n** (.) **stuff**
an' but we had some fun.
4. Julie: Um//hm.
5. Crystal: Went out sailing **an' stuff**.
6. Julie: Wull good.

Crystal's repeated use of *and stuff* marks a general assumption that
Julie will understand what she is saying and will accept Crystal's
portrayal of the situation because Crystal and Julie are longtime
friends who share not only experiences, but also goals and values. By
describing her current love interest to Julie, it may be that Crystal is
looking for some kind of reassurance that she's not making a mistake
by getting involved with this younger guy. She offers reasons why,
even though Frederico is young, her involvement with him is not a
bad idea, including: *he's super mature for his age*, he's *had a lot of
experiences*, and they are *really taking it slow*. Throughout the
conversation, Julie demonstrates her understanding (*Mmhm*) and provides supportive feedback (*Wull good*).

For some speakers, the use of *and stuff* has become not just frequent
but habitual. Consider the following excerpt, from an interview with
a U.S. soldier about the U.S. military's role in Haiti.

[10] We provided equipment to the Haitians, **and stuff**, we
provided security **and stuff**, we took care of people who
needed help **and stuff**. (*Windward O'ahu News*, Jul. 1995)

Just as *y'know* has become an almost reflex marker for "I don't have to
tell you everything because we share knowledge" (positive politeness), so too is *and stuff* developing a similar function for some speakers. Here the soldier uses the form *and stuff* almost reflexively to
mark invited solidarity as interactive partner.

A second and more exaggerated version of this usage of *an' stuff* is
offered in excerpt [11], from a conversation between nurses in the staff
lounge of a hospital emergency room. Here, Karen is discussing her
son's malformed chest, or *pectus excavatum*:

[11] 1. Karen: Yeah, I was real conce::rned, **you know**, (it'd
affect 'im)
2. Sharlene: What about the organs?
3. Karen: Yeah, right, see I: was real conce:rned we're
gonna have a pro:blem
4. Sharlene: (*) grow, yeah.
5. Karen: But (.) **y'know 'n stuff**, as he got a little bit
o::lder **'n stuff**, **y'know** doctor told me (***) and Justin
was fi::ne and has no problem. But as he's gotten older
you can see he's (.) he's flattening ou:t (.) **y'know, an'**

stuff , an' he:'s uh, his muscles are developing **'n 'stuff**,
and I even run my hand across his chest **y'know** and I
can tell it's fla̱tter. **Y'know**, so he's, yeah,
6. Donna: Pectus, does that curl i̱:n?
7. Karen: Yeah. Pectus is in, yeah.

Note the repeated co-occurrence of *and stuff* with *y'know* in excerpt
[11]. This offers additional support for the notion that these forms
share a common function—to mark invited solidarity as interactive
partner.

A distinctive feature of *an' stuff*, when used in this way as a
general marker of solidarity, is that it need not be attached to propo-
sitional information. Extract [12], from the same speaker, includes a
turn (line 7) that only has *Yeah an' stuff* or agreement and solidarity.

[12] 1. Karen: So (1.0) a::nyway, no I sta—I sa—I got out of
here by a quarter till yesterday **an' stuff**. I didn't (1.0)
see that la̱st patient.
2. Donna: You mean quarter to four.
3. Karen: Yeah, **an' stuff** —a̱fter I took care—a̱fter I took
care of the body, so. I just figured I didn't wanna leave
that ha//nging till the evening shift.
4. Donna: Now we kne::w him, didn't we?
5. Karen: Yea::h
6. Donna: 'Cause I 'member with his na:me.
7. Karen: Yeah **an' stuff** // He was—
8. Donna: He didn't lo̱ok familiar, but I mean in his
condition::, hhh.
9. Karen: No. He was a nice—he // was a ni̱ce—patient

Given this pattern of use, it is possible that the form *an' stuff* may be
in the process of migrating from its more typical clause-final position
to many other positions within utterances.

Disjunctive General Extenders as Hedges

Having noted how the adjunctive general extender *and stuff* appears
to function as a strategy of positive politeness, I can now consider how
a disjunctive general extender (e.g., *or something, or anything, or
whatever*) may indicate a strategy of negative politeness. When used
in certain types of utterances, these expressions seem to function as
"hedges" which reduce the speaker's risk of threatening the hearer's
face. Consider the exchange in [13].

[13] 1. Sara: Okay, lemme—lemme—lemme spell it out for
you, this is what I:: would ideally like to do.

2. Roger: Uh huh=
3. Sara: =I'd like to move out there 'n take over your apartment
4. Roger: Right
5. Sara: an' all the stuff that's in it an' just b<u>u</u>y it from you, **or whatever**, an' maybe like b<u>u</u>y your truck **or something**. I dunno.
6. Roger: Uh huh . . .

In this example, Sara's utterance in turns 3 and 5 (*I'd like to move out there 'n take over your apartment an' all the stuff that's in it an' just b<u>u</u>y it from you, or whatever, an' maybe like b<u>u</u>y your truck or something*) constitutes a proposal. As such, it represents a speaker's potentially imposing on a hearer. Since agreement to the proposal would involve compliance on the part of the hearer, and would potentially impose on the hearer, Sara's utterance may be considered a potentially face-threatening act. Given that Sara's utterance has that potential, it seems plausible that the general extenders *or whatever* and *or something* in [13] are functioning to express tentativeness. The modal adverb *maybe* and the succeeding utterance of *I dunno* confirm this interpretation. By emphasizing that what precedes the general extender represents just one possibility, Sara expresses only a weak commitment to the proposal being made. She signals that there may be alternatives (without necessarily having any particular alternatives in mind).

Excerpts [14]–[16] contain additional examples of disjunctive general extenders that function as hedges addressed to negative politeness. In each case, a speaker is in danger of imposing his or her wants on the hearer, thereby impeding the hearer's freedom of action, and consequently threatening negative face (see Brown and Levinson 1987: 65–66). To compensate, the speaker exhibits a face-saving act oriented to the hearer's negative face by adhering to two fundamental rules of politeness: (1) Don't impose; and (2) Give options (see R. Lakoff 1973: 298; Overstreet and Yule 1999a).

In [14], Julie and Donna are discussing their plans for the evening. Donna works in town near Julie's residence, and she isn't sure if she should drive home (out of town) and back before going out with Julie and her husband that night. Julie invites Donna to come straight to her house after work. She suggests that before they go out, they could *go for a walk or something*:

[14] 1. Julie: Come over an' hang out.
      2. Donna: 'kay.
      3. Julie: We can always, y'know, (1.0) just ya:ck an' have dinner.

4. Donna: Okay.
5. Julie: A//n' we could even go
6. Donna: (But—)
7. Julie: for a walk **or somethin'** // if ya wanna go—
8. Donna: Do I need to bring anything?

It might be argued that the general extender in turn 7 is used to refer to "types of exercise." However, as was the case in excerpt [13], the speaker is in a position of potentially imposing her wishes on the hearer if she proposes only "go for a walk." By employing the general extender *or something*, Julie marks *a walk* as just one option, and she indicates her willingness to entertain other possibilities (and not necessarily "types of exercise"). A similar interpretive issue involving the same expression was highlighted in the quote from Seinfeld that introduced chapter 2.

In excerpt [15], Sara and Roger are on a long-distance phone call. Sara expresses a desire to see Roger and his wife when they arrive in the town where Sara lives.

[15] 1. Sara: An uh uh—I'll see ya:: (.) I—may talk to y'all
            sometime next week, but if not, I'll see y'all Friday a—
            probably Friday afternoon=Friday evening when y'all
            get in
     2. Roger: Okay.=
     3. Sara: =I know y'all 'll be real tired, but (.5) hopefully
            we'll like hookup **or something.** // .hhh
     4. Roger: Sure.=
     5. Sara: =An' uh I'll talk to you (.) la//ter
     6. Roger: All right.

Since the fulfillment of Sara's expressed wish would involve compliance on Roger's part (and potentially impose on the hearer), Sara's basic proposition, *We'll hook up*, is potentially face-threatening. In combination with the other indicators, *hopefully* and *like*, the general extender *or something* can be seen to express tentativeness and to serve as a hedge addressed to the negative politeness consideration "Don't impose."

Finally, in excerpt [16], Julie is asking her mother about having her mail forwarded to a new address.

[16] 1. Julie: You know those mailing address cards where you
            change an address?
     2. Jean: Yeah, you get 'em at the post office.
     3. Julie: Yeah, I know that. Um, what was I gonna ask you

(.) If I put my name on (.) saying the stuff should go to
Louisiana, do you think they'll start sending your mail
to Louisiana? (.5) 'Cause we have the same last name.
(2.0)
4. Jean: Wull no, 'cause you're gonna put your own name
   on it—I don't thi:::nk
5. Julie: That's what I'm worried about.
6. Jean: Wull write down at the bottom "Please note"
   huh huh **or somethin'**
7. Julie: I don't know if it's worth it or whether I should—
   I probably won't get very much.

In turn 6, Jean makes a suggestion: *Wull write down at the bottom "Please note huh huh or somethin'."* In terms of politeness, Jean's suggestion that Julie take a specific course of action may be seen to impede Julie's freedom of action. The general extender here (*or something*) once again functions as a hedge addressed to a politeness strategy such as "Don't put pressure on the hearer to do (or refrain from doing) the act A" (Brown and Levinson 1987: 65–66). With regard to this example, it is also worth noting that Jean begins her utterance with *Wull*. As noted by Brown and Levinson, the particle *well* often occurs as a hesitation marker prior to a dispreferred response, or something that is potentially face-threatening. It may be that, in this case, Jean signals with *wull* that she is in danger of performing a potentially face-threatening act.

As the preceding examples suggest, disjunctive general extenders frequently occur in speech events involving invitations, offers, proposals, or requests. The following examples of a request [17] and an offer [18] were cited by other researchers.

[17] Could we, when you give us our essays back, and give us
titles could we sort of meet **or something**
(Channell 1994: 135)

[18] P: Wul lissid—(.) uh:: d'you wah me uh to come down'n
   getche t'//morrow **er anything**
   A: No: de:ar. (Davidson 1984: 107)

Since in making an offer (or an invitation, a proposal, or a request), a speaker creates the possibility of rejection (see Davidson 1984), the speaker's face in such contexts is also potentially at risk. Thus, in using a general extender to implicate options and express tentativeness, a speaker not only addresses the hearer's face concerns but also takes a step to "save" his or her own face.

Encouraging a Preferred Response

As Levinson (1983) notes, interlocutors tend to avoid creating contexts that would elicit dispreferred responses. It may be that, by using a general extender to implicate alternative possibilities, a speaker makes an offer, suggestion, or request less specific and thereby increases the likelihood of receiving a preferred response (i.e., acceptance). In the event that the hearer does not find the stated offer, suggestion, or request desirable, the hearer may choose to "accept" an alternative possibility which might have been implicated by the general extender. With this in mind, it is interesting to note that disjunctive general extenders often occur in what Davidson refers to as "subsequent versions of invitations and offers" (1984: 121). Consider excerpt [19].

[19] FIRST VERSION   A: hh You could meet me at U.C.Be:
                        an' I could show yih some 'a the other
                        things on the
     MONITOR SPACE   compu:ter, (.)
     SUBS. VERSION   maybe even teach yuh how tuh
                        program Ba:sic **er something.** .hhh
     RESPONSE   B: Wul I don' know if I'd wanna get
                        all that invo:lved, hh. hhh! (.hh)
                        (Davidson 1984: 121)

In [19], the speaker produces a first version of an offer. Then, following a pause in which there is no response from the hearer (which is taken as an indication of an impending dispreferred), the speaker produces a subsequent version of the offer which contains a general extender. By using the general extender *er something* to implicate alternative possibilities, the speaker makes the offer less specific, thereby increasing the likelihood of receiving a preferred response (i.e., acceptance). A second example of this is found in excerpt [20].

[20] A: We:ll dih you wan(na) me tuh (me) tuh jus' pick you ken
     you:—get intuh Robinson's suh yih could buy a li'l pair a
     slippers?
     (0.2)
     A: I mean or ken I getchu something?=**Er: somp'n?**=Er
     somp'n? hh! (Davidson 1984: 105)

In this example, the speaker says *er somp'n* twice. It appears that, for this speaker, the general extender has a major impact on what is communicated. By repeating the form, the speaker emphasizes other possibilities, in an attempt to make the offer more attractive to the hearer.

An interesting observation with regard to [19] and [20] is that, in using a general extender to indicate possible alternatives, the speaker may not actually be in a position to offer any others. An excellent example of this is presented in [21], from an episode of *My So-called Life*, an American television show about the life of a teenage girl. Here, the singer of Jordan's band, the Frozen Embryos, has just quit, and Jordan is worried that his band won't find a replacement.

[21] 1. Angela: You'll find someone somehow.
2. Jordan: Yeah, right.
3. Angela: So listen, this is probably a really stupid idea, but would Frozen Embryos ever want a girl—I mean like to sing—I—like—Rayanne Graf **or something**?
4. Jordan: Rayanne? Graf.

In proposing that Rayanne Graf might replace the singer of Jordan's band, Angela has only one person in mind. She is doing a favor for her friend Rayanne, who wants to sing in the band but does not know the band members very well. Because Angela has a serious crush on Jordan and does not know how well Rayanne can sing, she is reluctant to make the proposal on Rayanne's behalf. Angela uses the general extender *or something* to express tentativeness about the proposal. As it turns out, her tentativeness is warranted: Jordan responds with both skepticism and disbelief (*Rayanne? Graf.*).

Of course, not all examples of disjunctive general extenders that function as hedges occur within utterances that have the potential to threaten another's face (e.g., offers, suggestions, requests, or proposals). Hedges function generally as cautious notes and are not restricted to politeness strategies. Some other type of interpersonal expectation may be at risk, as demonstrated in excerpt [22].

[22] 1. Jim: U::m my new roommate has gotten me a new e-mail account at the U.H.
2. Cathy: O:::h
3. Jim: So um // uh
4. Cathy: How'd he do that?
5. Jim: He's got two: He's in the comp—He's in u:m engineering **or something like that**. // He works with computers
6. Cathy: Oh // wo:w
7. Jim: an' whatnot.

In turn 5, Jim makes a statement that communicates information about his roommate: *He's in u:m engineering or something like that.* In such cases, the use of a disjunctive general extender may serve as a hedge of a slightly different kind. Exploring the function of this kind of hedge will be the focus of chapter 8.

The Maxim of Quality
and Disjunctive General Extenders

Butt-head: Why is he, like, walkin' funny?
Beavis: Maybe he has HAMMEROIDS or somethin'.

(Marvel Comics, 1994)

In the excerpt above, the cartoon characters Beavis and Butt-head are talking about their school principal. While these characters may show no respect for most social norms, they do respect some basic principles of cooperative conversation. When Beavis wants to refer to a phenomenon he isn't sure of (*hammeroids*), he uses a general extender (*or somethin'*) to mark that lack of certainty. It is to this function of general extenders that we now turn.

In one of the most influential proposals concerning the nature of language use, Grice (1975) identified a set of assumptions which are presumed to be in effect in any cooperative interaction. These assumptions have been characterized by Levinson as "guidelines for the efficient and effective use of language in conversation to further co-operative ends" (1983: 101). In this chapter, I will explore how a speaker's use of a general extender may demonstrate both an orientation to one of these guidelines and an intention to adhere to it. First, however, it may be useful to consider the general principle of cooperation originally proposed by Grice, as well as the definition he gave for the maxim of Quality.

The Maxim of Quality

Grice (1975) presented a general concept, called the Cooperative Principle, as something that is assumed in all normal conversation, together with four sub-principles, called "maxims." In this chapter, I will only address the Maxim of Quality.

> *The Cooperative Principle*
> Make your conversational contribution such as is required,
> at the stage at which it occurs, by the accepted purpose or
> direction of the talk exchange in which you are engaged.

> *The Maxim of Quality*
> Try to make your contribution one that is true.
> 1. Do not say what you believe to be false.
> 2. Do not say that for which you lack adequate evidence.
> (1975: 45–46)

The requirements of Quality would lead conversational partners to assume a high degree of truth and certainty about what is being claimed in the course of an interaction. Indeed, as Horn has noted, "unless Quality . . . obtains, the entire conversational . . . apparatus collapses" (1984: 12). However, it is to be expected that, even when speakers are oriented to the second part of the maxim and wish to observe it, they will occasionally find themselves in danger of not adhering to the maxim. Among the devices for marking such occasions is the disjunctive general extender.

Quality Hedges

It appears that disjunctive general extenders (most typically *or something*) are often used as hedges on the Gricean Maxim of Quality, or the basic assumption that what we say will be accurate and based on good evidence. Maxim hedges, as defined by Brown and Levinson (1987: 166), mark the speaker's commitment to the maintenance of cooperation, while not strictly adhering to the requirements of the maxim. A hedge on the Maxim of Quality works in the following way: a speaker may assert something that he or she thinks is potentially inaccurate (in danger of not strictly adhering to the Maxim of Quality), but the speaker indicates in some conventional way a lack of commitment to the necessary truth of the content of the utterance, or part of the utterance—thus maintaining cooperation. By using a disjunctive general extender such as *or something* to indicate that the content of the message represents a best guess, or an approximation, a speaker can indicate potential noncompliance with the expectation of strict accuracy. This modifying or approximating function of some general extenders has been noted by other researchers, including Aijmer (1985), Ball and Ariel (1978), and Dines (1980).

As illustration, consider [1]. In this excerpt, the speakers are Julie and Crystal, two women in their thirties who have been friends since high school. They are talking about some of their former classmates.

[1] 1. Julie: I can't remember any ge—guys in our grade that were gay
    2. Crystal: Larry Brown an' an' John Murphy. // I—huh!
       I dunno, I heard John Murphy was dressed—was like a transvestite **or something.**
    3. Julie: You're kidding
    4. Crystal: I—I dunno. That was a—an old rumor, I don't even know if it was true.
    5. Julie: That's funny=
    6. Crystal: =Or cross-dresser // **or something**
    7. Julie: Larry—Larry Brown is ga::y?
    8. Crystal: No, I could see him doing that too, though.
       huh huh huh! I don't know wh(h)y: . . .

In this part of the conversation, Crystal is reporting second-hand information about a couple of guys from high school. Because the information is based on rumor, Crystal can't be sure whether or not it is true. In turn 2, Crystal says *I heard John Murphy was dressed—was like a transvestite or something.* The general extender *or something* in this utterance can be seen to suggest alternative possibilities, and thereby to function as a hedge on the truth of the statement. Note that in turn 4, Crystal explicitly states that she is not committed to the accuracy of the content of the utterance, by using expressions such as *I dunno* and *I don't even know if it was true.* In turn 6, Crystal goes on to offer another alternative—that John Murphy is *a cross-dresser.* Again, she follows her assertion with the hedge *or something.*

A second example of *or something* being used as a hedge on the accuracy of a statement is offered in excerpt [2]. Here Sara is telling Roger about her friends' plans to travel to New York and participate in a gay rights march.

[2] 1. Sara: Most of the people I know are goin' up the:re in (.) the end of Ju::ne for this big gay rights march i//t's
    2. Roger: Uh huh
    3. Sara: like the:: twenty fifth anniversary of the Sto:newall riots=I don't know if you've ever heard of the::m=
    4. Roger: =Um//um?

5. Sara: Uh—uh—anyway, like back in the sixties there
was an apartment complex called the Stonewall
apartments an' the::y—I'm not sure exactly what
happened either, but they ended up having these huge
riots there. An' it was like for (.) gay discrimination **or
something**=Anyway, this year is the twenty fifth
anniversary of it an' uh .hhhh So anywa::y
6. Roger: You thinking of going an' marching?
7. Sara: No, no, no.

During this conversation, Sara attempts to explain the cause of the
Stonewall riots, but she isn't sure of the facts. We know this because
she explicitly says so: *I'm not sure what happened either.* In turn 5,
she marks the utterance *an' it was like for gay discrimination* as
possibly inaccurate with the general extender *or something.*

A third example of a speaker using *or something* to hedge on the
Maxim of Quality is presented in [3]. The participants, Sara and
Maya, are talking about a mutual acquaintance of theirs, Doug.

[3] 1. Sara: He really looks a lot older than he did. I guess
2. Maya: Yeah he does.
3. Sara: traveling around London with (.) the—the
elephant Kellie Simpson would do that to you.
4. Maya: Oh, is that what he was doin'?
5. Sara: Yeah. He went to Lon//don
6. Maya: Oh ma:n=
7. Sara: =to live with he:r. I think they must've broke up
or something 'cause he's back no//w.
8. Maya: Yeah, they must've.

In turn 7, Sara speculates on the reason for Doug's return from London: *I
think they must've broke up or something.* Sara marks a lack of
commitment to the accuracy of her assertion with *think* (i.e., not
know), the epistemic modal *must've*, and the general extender *or
something*.[1]

It is interesting to note that, when the hearer is in a position to
judge the accuracy of the speaker's assertion, the hearer may interpret the hedge (*or something, or whatever*) as an invitation to offer
an assessment of its accuracy, or to collaborate in producing a more
accurate statement. For example, in [3], Maya responds to Sara's *I
think they must've broke up or something* with *Yeah, they must've.*
Further illustration of this is offered in excerpt [4], where Sara and
Maya continue their discussion of Doug's appearance.

[4] 1. Maya: He—he always looks like (.) he has really bad
bedhead (.5) now that he's got more hair or less hair **or**

something // (He's—)
2. Sara: He's got like more hair.

Here, Maya speculates on the causes of Doug's *bedhead*, saying it's due to the fact that *he's got more hair or less hair*, but indicating her lack of certainty with *or something*. Sara knows the person Maya is describing, and she responds to the hedge (*or something*) by offering her assessment *He's got like more hair*.

When disjunctive general extenders function as a hedge on the content of an utterance, they are frequently found in collocation with expressions such as *I don't know, maybe, probably, I can't remember, I'm not sure,* and *I think*.

Approximations

In many cases, a disjunctive general extender (typically *or something* or *or whatever*) functions to mark an utterance, or part of an utterance, not just as potentially inaccurate, but as an approximation. In this section, I will look at how speakers use these expressions to mark amounts, lexical items, and reported speech as approximations that may not meet strict expectations of accuracy.

Amounts: Ten pounds er somethin'

The use of *or something* and *or whatever* as markers of approximation is particularly clear where numbers or amounts precede the general extender. As illustration, consider excerpts [5]–[7]. In extract [5], from Guthrie's data, a female speaker (S) is talking about how she and her boyfriend used to pick and sell psilocybin mushrooms.

[5]   S: every (.) spring we used ta go to <u>Dallas</u> an' visit some
           friends cruise down outside ya know like around
           <u>Houston</u> pick psilocybin mushrooms=
      A: =Um hmm
      S: An' every year ya know pick ten pounds **er somethin'**
           bring 'em back.   (Guthrie 1994: 84)

In using the general extender *er somethin'*, S marks the named amount (*ten pounds*) as an estimate, which may not be exactly right. By hedging on the accuracy of her statement, S is able to offer an approximate amount without risking a violation of the Maxim of Quality.

In excerpt [6], the speaker is talking about the amount of vacation time her father gets each year.

[6]   B: for that job he gets—I think it's three weeks or a month
      or something of vacation every year.
      (Craig and Tracy 1983: 306)

In fact, B isn't sure exactly how much time her father gets off. She estimates that it's between three and four weeks. Once again, the general extender *or something* allows her to offer a best guess at the amount without being absolutely certain.

Finally, in [7], Sara (in Louisiana) is asking Roger (in Hawai'i) whether she will need a Hawai'i driver's license to open a bank account there.

[7]   Sara: Because I know when I:: first moved down here in like
      (.) what? nineteen eighty-six **or whatever,** um I had to go
      get a Louisiana driver's license before they would let me
      open a bank account.

Sara states that she needed a state license before, when she opened an account in Louisiana. She pauses in the middle of her utterance, and searches for the date of her move to Louisiana (*what?*) before naming it: *nineteen eighty-six.* The fact that Sara hesitates and conducts a search for the date suggests that she is unsure of it. The general extender *or whatever* follows the date and marks it as an approximation, or best guess. Note that while *or something* and *or whatever* are both employed as hedges on the accuracy of statements, there is a subtle distinction between these expressions. *Or whatever* seems to carry an added implication of "it doesn't matter." This observation will receive further attention later in this chapter.

Lexical items: HAMMEROIDS or somethin'

In the excerpt at the beginning of this chapter, Beavis uses *or somethin'* to mark a preceding lexical item as a word he isn't quite sure of: *Maybe he's got HAMMEROIDS or somethin'.* The word we assume Beavis intends here is "hemorrhoids." Where disjunctive general extenders are used to hedge on the accuracy of a lexical item like this, the lexical item may be close to correct, or an approximation.

Some additional examples of general extenders that appear to mark preceding lexical items as approximate are presented in excerpts [8]–[9]. In excerpt [8], the speaker (Ernie) is conducting a name search.

[8]   Ernie: I said no I know his name is something else. Teddy 'r
      Tom **'r somethin.**   (Jefferson 1990: 66)

In this instance, it seems that the name Ernie is searching for begins with a *T* and is perhaps one or two syllables in length; it may or may not be one of the two names mentioned.

A second example of a disjunctive general extender as a hedge on the accuracy of a lexical item is presented in [9]. The point of interest is where B says *collate or something.*

[9] B: that one type then there's an operation test they're
          interested say in well particularly seeing various
          adverbs and they write something like I entirely dot
          dot dot and the student has to complete the sentence
     A: m
     B: well with entirely they'll nearly all write agree with
          you
     A: yes
     B: and entirely and agree
     A: m
     B: go together
     A: m
     B: collate **or something** it's called
     A: yea
     B: (laughs) and then they in fact try another adverb
          (Svartvik and Quirk 1980: 136)

It appears that the word B intends here is *collocate*. Once again, the named item (*collate*) is used, but it is marked by the speaker as an attempt to say the correct form which may not be exactly right.

The use of *or something* to mark a lexical item as approximately right is not all that new. In excerpt [10], from the novel *Persuasion*, a character uses the general extender *or something very like it* to indicate that the name *Wentworth* may not be exactly right, but that it is probably close.

[10] When the Crofts called this morning (they called here
       afterwards, did not they?) they happened to say, that her
       brother, Captain Wentworth, is just returned to England, or
       paid off, **or something**, and is coming to see them almost
       directly; and most unluckily it came into mamma's head,
       when they were gone, that Wentworth, **or something very
       like it**, was the name of poor Richard's captain, at one
       time, I do not know when or where, but a great while before
       he died, poor fellow! (Austen 1818/1961: 52)

In fact, disjunctive general extenders are used twice in this passage as hedges on the Maxim of Quality. In the first instance, the general extender *or something* is used to indicate that the speaker is unsure about the details of a report given by the Crofts earlier that morning.

Reported Speech: "Leave Henry" or something

Another context in which the general extender *or something* is commonly found is the environment following quoted speech or thought, as in excerpts [11]–[12]. In each of these excerpts, Donna is telling her friend Blake about an argument she had with her husband, Henry. The underlying cause of the conflict was that Donna felt neglected, and Henry thought she needed too much attention. In excerpt [11], Donna is telling Blake about the point at which Henry complained that she was always demanding attention.

[11] 1.   Donna: He was saying how I—I'll say "He::::y,
          nobody::::'s listening to me::::::" **or something** an'
          I said // I don't
     2.   Blake: You d<u>o:</u> do that

Donna dramatizes Henry's imitation of her by talking in a whiny voice and lengthening her syllables. In fact, Henry may not have represented Donna's talk in that manner at all. But Donna is not in danger of violating the Maxim of Quality: She uses the general extender *or something* to mark the quoted material as an approximation, or as one of a number of possible things, similar in form and content, that could have been said.

In excerpt [12], Donna tells Blake about how Henry reacted when she suggested that they separate for a while.

[12] 1.   Donna: Now he thinks it's because I talked to Malia
          and Malia told me like "Leave Henry" **or something,**
          an' I said
     2.   Blake: Did she?=
     3.   Donna: =No::::. I talked, Malia listened, and she said,
          "Well, those are things to think about."

Apparently, Henry thought Donna's sister Malia had advised Donna to leave the relationship. This hadn't happened. The utterance in turn 1 (*"Leave Henry"*), followed by the general extender *or something*, represents an approximation, or one of a number of possible things, similar in form and content, which, according to Donna, Henry imagined was said.[2]

As Tannen (1989) has pointed out, reported dialogue is almost always reconstructed and hence is typically inaccurate, yet it is frequently employed by speakers in an effort to dramatize their narratives. Reporting talk is consequently a common context in which the general extender *or something (like that)* is employed as a means of marking potential inaccuracy. The following excerpt is from a written narrative, a novel about the Simpson trial. In this passage, the speaker is reporting what O. J. Simpson said before he made lewd gestures to a young girl seated next to him at a dinner party.

[13] On his other side was this heavenly little blond girl who was a friend of one of Louis and Noonie's daughters—I can't remember her name—and O. J. said to me, "I'm going to hit on her," **or something like that**, and it sounded innocent and cute. (Dunne 1997: 12)

The speaker isn't sure exactly what O. J. said, but he knows it was something along the lines of "I'm going to hit on her." In using the general extender *or something* to mark the utterance as approximate, the speaker can give the audience a much more dramatic version of the event by having them hear what was said, while still adhering to the Maxim of Quality.

Analogies: Jurassic Park or something

There are times when we have unusual or novel experiences which are difficult to describe to others. In an effort to communicate what these experiences are like, we compare them to something we assume is known to our interlocutor. Consider the following example from a newspaper article. Here, a motorist describes his trip on a new sixteen-mile freeway which winds through an undeveloped valley on the island of O'ahu in Hawai'i.

[14] It was wonderful. It was like a drive through Jurassic Park **or something**. (*Honolulu Advertiser*, 14 Dec. 1997)

In an attempt to describe his experience driving over the new freeway, the motorist says *it was like a drive through Jurassic Park*, the setting of a blockbuster movie by the same title, which is widely known among members of his American culture. The general extender *or something* marks this as an analogy that approximates what the experience was like but doesn't capture it completely.

When experiences are more abstract, speakers are often quite creative in their analogies. Consider excerpts [15] and [16]. In [15], a man describes a physical sensation he had while driving his car, just before he lost consciousness and critically injured a pedestrian.

[15] I started feeling something in my throat or stomach, like something was boiling in my stomach **or something**. (Honolulu Advertiser, 10 Aug. 1997)

As it turns out, this man's experience was caused by a new medication he was taking that caused strange and dangerous side effects.

Clearly, he does not expect that his interlocutor will have experienced something boiling in her stomach. In using the general extender *or something*, the man appeals to an intersubjective understanding of what that might feel like, and he thus marks the analogy as an attempted approximation.

Finally, in excerpt [16], from a novel, a character with a drug problem describes his emotions after being caught on a serious cocaine binge.

[16] I feel like such a moron. I'm so ashamed. Here I am way out
in the middle of my life and I feel like this. It's like I've
got wind blowing through my chest **or something**. (Fisher
1987: 92)

In an attempt to describe what we might assume is an intense feeling of emptiness, the character makes an analogy and marks it as an approximation of how he felt.

Jokes: Rubber Panties or something

Given their role in marking the possibly non-accurate status of accompanying information, it should not be surprising that disjunctive general extenders (typically *or something*) occur strategically in cartoons and jokes. In these environments, they signal to the hearer that what precedes the general extender is not accurate or real. Instead, it is a purposeful exaggeration, or an analogy, which should not be taken too literally. Consider [17], in which Sara is joking about the condition of Roger's old pick-up truck, which she has been driving.

[17] 1.   Sara: Th—that truck makes the most amazing sno̱rting
              noises // sometimes
     2.   Roger: huh huh huh
     3.   Sara: like when you're goin' up a hill,
     4.   Roger: Right.=
     5.   Sara: =it makes a noise exactly—it sounds exactly like
              (.) I dunno like a do̱::g or a ho̱:rse **or something** like like
              when it's when it's u::h discontent. heh heh heh It
              m(h)akes the str(h)angest noise—everytime it does I
              just bust out laughing.
     6.   Roger: huh huh huh ha::::h=okay

The humorous analogy in turn 5 (*like a dog or a horse or something*) is marked by Sara's laughter immediately after it and Roger's laughing response in turn 6.

A second example of a joke with *or something* is presented in excerpt [18], from an interview with the comedian Robin Williams:

[18] Williams obviously gets a kick out of the shots at the right wing, especially when the fictional co-chairman of the "Coalition for Moral Values" gets caught in a rather compromising position. "Every so often, that sense of righteous indignation gets blown apart when some of these guys are found wearing rubber panties **or something**," he says. "You know, they say, 'I was just diving.'" (*USA Weekend*, 1–3 March 1996)

Williams uses the general extender *or something* to indicate that the scenario he is describing is fictional, and he is not committed to the accuracy of the statement. Instead, this outlandish scenario (*these guys are found wearing rubber panties*) is intended to be absurd and humorous.

Excerpt [19] is from a newspaper article about the superhuman homemaker and handywoman Martha Stewart.

[19] In one of her shows, she took fresh eggs from the hens she raised and made a meal to rival the Last Supper. Ten minutes later she painted a colored diamond on her porch (exhausting just to watch). While the paint was drying, I think she built a house **or something**.   (*Honolulu Advertiser*, 5 Jan. 1997)

The writer of this article uses the general extender *or something* to mark his assertion (*While the paint was drying, I think she built a house*) as a purposeful exaggeration which is intended to be humorous and not to be taken literally.

Occasionally a writer specifically marks the use of an exaggerated analogy as humorous. In extract [20], the writer uses the verb *laughed* to describe the function of the bus driver's comment, ending in *or something*.

[20] "Can you imagine" the woman said, "it's even illegal to own a spotted owl. You can do time for it." "Like kidnappin' a baby **or somethin**" laughed the bus driver. (Codrescu 1994: 252)

The basic structure of the bus driver's comment in [20] appears to have become almost formulaic for the use of *or something* as a hedge on Gricean Quality. The formulaic construction *like X or something* occurs in many examples presented so far in this chapter—[1], [2], [7], [12], [14], [15], [16], [17], and [20]. It also occurs in the example illustrated in figure 8.1.

Given their uses in jokes and humorous exaggerations, it is to be expected that disjunctive general extenders such as *or something* will

THE FAR SIDE   By GARY LARSON

"Gad, it gives me the creeps when he does that.
I swear that goldfish is possessed or something."

Figure 8.1. Goldfish. (The Far Side © 1985 Farworks, Inc.
Used by permission of Universal Press Syndicate. All rights reserved.)

also occur in cartoons and cartoon captions. From the many examples I
have noted, two illustrations are presented here as figures 8.1 and 8.2.

Unimportant details: *I feel your pain or whatever*

Although it appears with less frequency, the related structure *like X
or whatever* may also have a function that is similar to the approximating uses of the structure already described with *or something*.
Both constructions appear in extract [21], from a telephone conversation between Sara and Roger. Sara is telling Roger about her annoyance with her mother's recently expressed worries regarding Sara's
planned move to Hawai'i.

[21] 1. Sara: My mom was tellin' me last night—She watched
          some stupid fuckin' show on .hhh (.) like Haw—w—
          Waikiki five O, **or something**, I dunno=There was some
          stupid ass like ne:w detective show or
      2. Roger: Uh // huh
      3. Sara: like horror show, or so//ap opera, **or whatever**
      4. Roger: huh huh huh huh huh
      5. Sara: that's s—set in fuckin' Waikiki. An' so my mom
          calls me this evening an' says "I watched this show
          last night an' there were these (.) o—oriental girls who
          wound up givin' up a kidney . . . "

As has already been noted, there is a subtle distinction between the
use of *or something* and *or whatever*. Whereas *or something* may simply mark a preceding element (i.e., the correct name of the show) as
an approximation in turn 1 of [21], *or whatever* adds an additional
implication of "it doesn't actually matter whether certain details are
exactly correct" in a particular context. We can characterize this
general extender, *or whatever*, as having a dismissive quality, in
addition to its marking potential non-accuracy. In turns 1 and 3 of [21],
Sara is having difficulty with the appropriate description of what
to her was "a stupid ass . . . show," and she ends her attempt with *or
whatever*, signaling both the approximating and the dismissive
nature of her description. The larger context of Sara's annoyance is
revealed in turn 5: the irrelevant television show has caused her
mother to worry about her safety.

Calvin and Hobbes   by Bill Watterson

Figure 8.2. (Calvin and Hobbes © 1995 Watterson. Dist. by Universal
Press Syndicate. Reprinted with permission. All rights reserved.)

Within a given context, *or whatever* will have different motivations according to the different reasons a speaker may have for deciding that certain details are unimportant. Consider excerpt [22], from a written text.

[22] What is relevant here is the parson's role as clergyman and custodian of the values of his religion rather than the fact that he is overweight, or near retirement, or unmarried, or plays golf, or rides a bicycle, or smokes a pipe, **or whatever**. (Widdowson 1996: 64)

On this occasion, *or whatever* occurs at the end of a list of things that the writer explicitly characterizes as not being relevant in that context.

In some cases, *or whatever* can be interpreted as indicating more than "unimportant details" and having the stronger and potentially negative implication of "I don't care." In excerpt [23], a commentator for National Public Radio is discussing presidential candidate Bob Dole's effort to shake the image of being a listless campaigner and to look as though he really cares, by producing sharper speeches and avoiding the use of the word *whatever*.

[23] Schorr: Y'know one of the interesting things about listening to Senator Dole is that he—his use of the word *whatever*, an—which he trails off, and says for example, as he said in one speech "I feel your pain, **or whatever**," which tended to make him look as though he wasn't serious about what he was saying. I don't think you'll hear many more *whatevers* from him from now on—I think they are trying to get him to look as though he really means everything he is saying. (*Weekend Edition*, 4 May 1996)

According to Schorr, Dole's use of the general extender *or whatever* communicated a sense of indifference or lack of concern about what he was saying (*I feel your pain*). An example such as [23] provides good evidence that some individuals are indeed aware of general extenders in use and, on certain occasions, of their powerful impact on what is conveyed. Senator Dole did not succeed in his bid to become president.

When it is used to mark an attitude of indifference to a preceding part of an utterance, we might say that the general extender *or whatever* has a downgrading effect. As we will see in the next chapter, this effect can also be noted with certain adjunctive general extenders. In chapter 9, I will continue to explore the interpersonal function of general extenders, focusing on how these expressions can be used as hedges on the Maxim of Quantity.

–9–

The Maxim of Quantity
and Adjunctive General Extenders

I'll probably be working at the Whole Foods, y'know, probably playing warehouses, hanging around places like the Radio Shack, screaming that I used to know you, an' you'll be there in the lights, all beautiful an' shit.

Reality Bites (1994)

The quotation above is from a point in the film *Reality Bites* when the speaker (Troy, the struggling musician) is telling Lelaina (the about-to-be-famous videographer) how things will be when she's a big success. He could have ended his comparison at the word *beautiful*. But he doesn't. There is more to his message, and the "more" is expressed by the general extender. In this chapter, I will take a look at how *an' shit* and a number of other adjunctive general extenders can be viewed as hedges on expectations arising from the Maxim of Quantity.

The Maxim of Quantity

In chapter 8, I focused on the use of disjunctive general extenders in relation to the Maxim of Quality, within the framework of Grice's (1975) Cooperative Principle of conversation. In this chapter, I will focus on the use of adjunctive general extenders in relation to the Maxim of Quantity from the same analytic framework. Grice's proposed Maxim of Quantity is expressed in the following way:

1. Make your contribution as informative as is required (for the current purposes of the exchange).

2. Do not make your contribution more informative than is required. (1975: 45)

As many writers (e.g., Horn 1984) have pointed out, the two parts of this maxim are like two forces pulling the speaker in opposite directions. In earlier proposals, such as those of Zipf (1949) and Martinet (1962), the first part ("say a lot") was seen as the speaker's need to communicate a message fully, and the second part ("say a little") was described as the speaker's desire to "restrict his output of energy, both mental and physical, to the minimum compatible with achieving his ends" (Martinet 1962: 139). In more recent approaches, such as Relevance Theory (Sperber and Wilson 1995), the same two forces continue to be treated as fundamental.

The speaker's task, in adhering to the Maxim of Quantity, is to achieve an effective compromise between the two forces. In accomplishing that task, the speaker will sometimes need to mark that what is actually being said may not be exactly in line with expectations associated with the Maxim of Quantity. On such occasions, adjunctive general extenders appear to be extremely useful devices.[1]

Quantity Hedges

In their discussion of what they call "Quantity hedges," Brown and Levinson list a number of English expressions "which give notice that not as much or not as precise information is provided as might be expected" (1987: 166). Their list, including expressions such as *roughly, more or less,* and *approximately,* is focused mainly on the hedges oriented to lack of precision or "not as precise . . . as might be expected." If we focus instead on the other aspect, "not as much . . . as might be expected," we would anticipate finding English expressions that allow the speaker to indicate that there is more information, but it is not being provided at that time.

The most fundamental message of an adjunctive general extender is "there is more." Given this basic message, adjunctive general extenders are perfectly suited to the role of hedges on the Maxim of Quantity. Indeed, there are many different versions of adjunctive general extenders available for any occasion when the message "there is more" needs to be marked.

In example [1], a woman is expressing her concern that she hasn't heard from a friend who is pregnant.

[1]   If she's gonna go through labor and delivery and she's
      gonna have a baby **and all this stuff** (.5) you know I'd like
      to be able to be there.

The general extender (*and all this stuff*) signals that, of course, there
is much more involved in the events surrounding a birth, but she won't
spell out any further details here. As already pointed out in chapter
5, a basic motivation for not being more "informative" is the intersubjective assumption, marked by *you know* in [1], that the unstated
information can be treated as shared knowledge.
      A similar use of *and stuff*, combining both elements ("there is
more" and "you know what I mean"), is found in example [2], from the
B–K conversation.

[2]   I was thinking of—an excuse to get away from exams and
      ((snickering)) papers **and stuff**   (Craig and Tracy 1983: 310)

In this example, one student is talking to another about a hot-air
balloon trip as a way of taking a break from the many demands of
college, not all of which are spelled out in detail. In example [3], it is
the demands of a medical emergency that are iconically expressed in
a rushed staccato rhythm, with no time to explain all the details (*all
the rest of it*).

[3]   he was in his forties and they thought ((noise)) heart
      attack. nine nine nine **all the rest of it**   (Cheepen and
      Monaghan 1990: 147)

Example [3] provides a particularly clear illustration of a general
extender covering "there is a lot more" and being motivated as a
hedge on Quantity because of the emergency situation (following *nine
nine nine*, the telephone number for emergency services in Britain).
      This use of general extenders is not restricted to talk about emer-
gencies. As Macaulay (1985) has noted, there are some individuals
whose speech style is characterized by a large number of general
extenders (called "tags" by Macaulay) signaling that a lot more could
be said. In his insightful analysis of the recorded speech of a former
coal miner (A. S.), Macaulay observes:

> In his use of tags, A. S. seems to be saying "I could be more
> precise if you wanted me to be so, but in the interests of
> brevity . . . ", and this would be consistent with the
> slightly pedantic tone to his speech, in which the most

> salient feature is his idiosyncratically frequent use of *et cetera*. (1985: 115)

According to Macaulay, this speaker is using general extenders in a way that almost exactly matches the description of Quantity hedges in Brown and Levinson (1987). Macaulay's other observation, that there may be a connection between using general extenders as hedges on Quantity and sounding slightly pedantic, can be supported by examples from the speech and writing of academics, as I will note later in this chapter.

Within the broader, public domain, adjunctive general extenders often appear in signs that display the names of businesses. Consider the signs represented as figures 9.1 and 9.2, which were found in Honolulu, Hawai'i. Each sign offers an example of what is sold in that place, followed by an adjunctive general extender which indicates that "there is more."

As noted in chapter 3, this seems to be a common practice among businesses that sell a novel selection of items, where it is difficult to represent what the store has to offer via a single lexicalized label such as *furniture*. Indeed, one of these businesses (*Futons, etc.*) sells an unusual assortment of furniture and furnishings, but primarily futons. The other (*Eggs 'n Things*) is a restaurant serving a large range of items that tend to be eaten (in Hawai'i) with eggs for breakfast. As necessarily happens with any instance of "there is more," the interpretation of the general extenders ("Will we sleep on the *etc.* or eat them?") in signs of this kind depends on a substantial amount of assumed socio-cultural (or experiential) background knowledge.

Adjunctive general extenders indicating "there is more information" can also be found in written discourse, as exemplified in excerpts [4]–[6]. Extract [4] is from an introduction to pragmatics.

[4]   Here, one encounters notions such as the "register"(allowing
       us to determine whether an utterance is to be considered
       formal or relaxed, whether or not it connotes social

Figure 9.1. Futons, etc. sign.

Figure 9.2. Eggs 'n Things sign.

prestige, **and so on**); the modal aspects of the utterance (having to do with speakers' and hearers' attitudes towards what is said); questions of rhetoric (e.g. 'how to get one's point across') and similar issues that have been almost totally neglected by linguistics (as they have been, until recently, by mainsteam philosophy ever since the demise of the Sophists); **and so on and so forth.** (Mey 1993: 31).

In this paragraph, the author uses *and so on* to indicate that there are more things involved in the analysis of register, and he concludes the discussion with *and so on and so forth*, indicating that there are many more issues in this area. The general extenders seem to solve the problem of being informative to a certain degree on the topic without going into too much detail. There is, however, another subtle message being communicated via forms such as *and so on* in expository prose of the type illustrated in [4]. They may actually be signaling a treatment of information that is not shared, as if it was shared. The message received may be that the author is actually marking that he knows "more." It could be this effect that gives a "slightly pedantic tone" (Macaulay 1985: 115) to double general extenders such as *and so on and so forth* in academic discourse.

Next, consider excerpt [5], from a memo addressed to members of a university department. The memo was written by the chairman of the department, who had fallen out of a tree over the weekend and wanted to excuse himself from attending an upcoming social function.

[5]   As fate will have it, over the weekend I fractured a rib, am
       bandaged up and under strong nauseating pain medication
       etc. etc. Therefore, I will be unable to attend.

The repeated general extender (*etc. etc.*) emphasizes that there is not only more, but *much* more that could be said here, but that the amount said is assumed to be sufficient for present purposes. By emphasizing that there is (*much*) more that could be said about his physical condition, the chairman adds strength to his excuse without having to specify what the "more" is.

A more widely recognized example of this usage is presented in excerpt [6], from the novel *Anna and the King of Siam*.

[6]   He pleased very much in and was playful of almost
       everything, some important, and some unimportant, as
       riding on Elephants and Horses and Ponies, racing of them
       and racing of rowing boats, firing on birds and beasts of
       prey, dancing and singing in various ways pleasantly, and
       various curiosity of almost everything, and music of almost
       every description, and in taming of dogs, monkeys, **&c.**, **&c.**,
       that is to say briefly that he has tested almost everything
       eatable except entirely testing of Opium and play. (Landon
       1944: 308)

In her description of the king, Landon writes that he "pleased very much in and was playful of almost everything, some important, and some unimportant." She goes on to name quite a number of activities as illustration, followed by the general extender *&c., &c.* (*et cetera, et cetera*). The repeated general extender after a long list of examples emphasizes that there are not only more, but *many* more examples that could be given here. For this writer, striking the balance between saying enough to communicate her message (the king had *many* interests), and not saying too much, is a bit tricky. She uses the general extender to indicate that what she is saying may not be exactly in line with the Maxim of Quantity. It appears she thinks she is in danger of saying too much, for immediately after the general extender, she attempts to *say briefly* what the king had done. In the film version of this story (*The King and I*) the king's frequent use of *et cetera* *et cetera* became a defining feature of his style and personality. He used this form in a flippant manner, as if to say "there is more, but I don't owe you any more information, for I am the king." For some observers, the department chairman quoted in [5] had developed a similarly autocratic use of *et cetera et cetera* in his spoken language. It may be that doubling this particular general extender marks the "more" as, in fact, information that won't be shared.

Shared worlds *an' that kinda thing*

The imperial use of *et cetera* for "there is more" is not common in casual conversation among familiars. As social actors assuming a shared world (Husserl 1929/1977), conversational partners can signal that, because of their intersubjective understanding, they do not need to express all details of events explicitly. In essence, the compromise between "say a lot" and "say a little" required by the Gricean Maxim of Quantity is signaled by the admission of "there is more" and its intersubjective subtext "but you know what I mean." Examples [7]–[10] provide some illustrations of this compromise in context.

In excerpt [7], Blake and Donna are in the kitchen preparing their dinner. Donna directs Blake to the cabinet containing spices and herbs and says:

[7] 1. Donna: There's garlic salt an' onion powder **an' things like (that)—**
    2. Blake: Okay.

Here Donna uses the expression *and things like that* to indicate that there are more items available in the cabinet than the ones she explicitly names. Blake's response (*Okay*) indicates that he considers Donna's abbreviated message to be sufficient.

As noted in chapter 3, speakers do not typically go on to state explicitly what was implicated by their use of an adjunctive general extender. In the rare instances when this does happen, it may be that the speaker supplies the additional information in an effort to supplement what is subsequently considered to be an insufficient contribution (i.e., one that is less informative than required, or assumes too much). As illustration, consider excerpt [8], previously presented in chapter 3.

[8] 1. Julie: Frederico, huh?
    2. Crystal: Frederico=I know! An' his brother is Juan. huh huh // huh

3. Julie: O:::h, look out!
4. Crystal: Juan is one of those light ones. He has red hair **an' everything.** L—Light hair, blue eyes, (.) white skin, Mex—um, uh Spanish, y'know.
5. Julie: Umhm

Note that Crystal does not receive any supportive feedback from Julie (in the form of backchannels) after her utterance of *and everything* in turn 4. Crystal subsequently elaborates on *He has red hair and everything*, saying *L—Light hair, blue eyes, (.) white skin, Mex—um, uh Spanish, y'know*. Crystal's description could be viewed as an example of minimization in an effort to accommodate the two parts of the Maxim of Quantity (Levinson 1987). According to Levinson, the procedure of minimization is interactionally achieved, and it works in the following way: "one can try a minimal form and see if it works, if not, escalate" (1987: 119). The minimal form (*red hair and everything*) is tried, and then a more elaborate description follows.

Another point of interest in this elaboration is Crystal's use of *y'know*. In addition to emphasizing the existence of shared knowledge with the hearer, *you know* (*y'know*) can also be used to check whether the hearer possesses some knowledge that is necessary for the currrent exchange (Schiffrin 1987). It may be that, in using *y'know* at this point, Crystal is checking to see whether she has provided enough information to convey her message to Julie. According to Schiffrin, it is crucial in such cases that the hearer "acknowledge his/her receipt of that information either by affirming that information . . . or by marking its reception with *oh*" (1987: 272). In this case, Julie acknowledges receipt of the information with *Umhm* in turn 5.

Now consider excerpt [9]. Rosie is telling Julie about a phone call she made to Frank, a guy she had been dating. Rosie had not heard from Frank in a couple of weeks, and despite some reservations, she had finally decided to call him.

[9] 1. Rosie: W—I didn't want him to think I was like (.) pining for him or anything.
2. Julie: Good.=
3. Rosie: =so I just hhheh said (.) "th<u>a</u>nk you for the check"
4. Julie: .hhh
5. Rosie: an' y'know, "I was just sayin' hi, an' seein' how your first day on the job was" **an' that kinda thing**,=
6. Julie: =Mmhm=
7. Rosie: =kept it really light.

In [9], Rosie's report of what she said to Frank is followed by *an' that kinda thing.* In using this general extender, Rosie marks the talk which precedes it as sufficient to convey her message to Julie, and she treats the "more" she said to Frank as sufficiently knowable. Of course, Rosie does not expect Julie to be able to infer exactly what was said. In using the adjunctive general extender, Rosie marks her assumption that, based on shared knowledge of the types of conversations people have, Julie will be able to recognize the type of conversation she had with Frank. (Rosie subsequently describes the conversation as *really light*).

A similar example is presented in excerpt [10]. In this exchange, Anne explains the content of an e-mail message she sent to Roger, which he is currently unable to retrieve. Anne had sent the message to congratulate Roger on his recent marriage.

[10] 1. Anne: Well you've got the gist of it—You'll see it. It just sorta says that's great I'm // thrilled
2. Roger: Right.
3. Anne: um // y'know
4. Roger: Okay
5. Anne: I'm happy you're happy stay happy
6. Roger: ⌐Right
7. Anne: ⌐Y'know. Be happy for everybody. It's like hhh. huh huh huh Go with it **an' all that stuff** and u://m
8. Roger: Uh huh (1.0)
9. Anne: have a good one.

Anne characterizes the e-mail message in turns 1 to 7; she then uses an adjunctive general extender (*an' all that stuff*) to mark the preceding instances as sufficient to convey the gist of her message. It appears that Anne is appealing to Roger's shared sense of what would be a socially appropriate reaction to the news of a friend's marriage. She offers examples of cliché expressions heard in social contexts, such as *Go with it* and *have a good one.* These utterances can be characterized as representing a kind of social routine, which, because of its script-like nature, is sufficiently predictable or knowable.

Note that in [8]–[10] the speakers mark their assumption of shared knowledge with *y'know.* Also, throughout these interactions, the hearers provide supportive feedback in the form of backchannels, indicating to the speakers that they understand the message. Indeed, it may be that in some cases, the occurrence of such positive backchannels prompts the speaker to use the general extender (i.e., the hearer is acting like she or he already understands).

Downgrading *and all that crap*

Instead of an assumption of shared knowledge or experience as a basis
for not strictly adhering to Maxim of Quantity, the speaker may indicate that the "more" that might be said has low value or, for any
number of reasons, is simply not worth the expenditure of communicative energy. The speaker can use an adjunctive general extender to
downgrade the information that is not being included and hence
provide a motivation for not fully following Quantity. As we will see,
the use of pejorative nouns within adjunctive general extenders is
often indicative of this downgrading process.

As pointed out in the discussion of example [10], adjunctive
general extenders may be used as a hedge on Quantity when the
"more" information represents a well-established and thus
predictable social routine. By using an adjunctive general extender
containing a pejorative noun, a speaker expresses a negative attitude
toward the predictable "more" which is considered tedious, boring,
trite, or perhaps insincere.

For example, consider excerpt [11]. In this exchange, Roger is
telling Sara that he'll talk to his landlord about allowing her to
take over his apartment when he moves out. Reasonably priced
apartments are hard to come by, and there may be some competition
for his place.

[11] 1. Roger: I will um intimate to the people who:: r̰ent me
          this place
      2. Sara: Uh huh
      3. Roger: that there is someone who will y'know=like (.)
          take it over, and under my recommendation as y'know—
          all that crap, .hhhh // an' um
      4. Sara: Yeah.

Roger offers to speak with his landlord on Sara's behalf, and he gives
her an idea of what he'll say: *there is someone who will y'know=like
(.) take it over, and under my recommendation as y'know—all that
crap.* In using the general extender *(and) all that crap*, Roger downgrades the "more" that is not included. We cannot be sure why Roger
is downgrading the "more" that he might have said. It may be that,
because the kind of talk involved in such procedures is routine and
predictable, he considers it unnecessary or boring to elaborate on it.

In more formal contexts, the form *et cetera* may be used to downgrade the "more" that is considered routine and predictable. For
example, the chairman of a university committee recently opened a
meeting with the utterance presented in [12].

[12] Hi, last meeting, Merry Christmas, **et cetera**

Aware that his obligatory greeting and seasonal good wishes are likely to be perceived as routine rather than heartfelt, the chairman used the general extender (*et cetera*) to cover the required sentiments here. In doing so, he may have been expressing mild contempt for such routines, which seem insincere or phony, and essentially inviting a similar reaction from his colleagues.

A similar sentiment is expressed by Holden Caulfield, perhaps the biggest anti-phony of all time, in the first lines of the novel *The Catcher in the Rye*. As a genuine individual attempting to recount a personal story in [13], Holden refuses to follow the standard formula for story-telling, which begins with a certain type of biographical information.

[13] If you really want to hear about it, the first thing you'll
        probably want to know is where I was born, and what my
        lousy childhood was like, and how my parents were occu-
        pied and all that before they had me, **and all that David
        Copperfield kind of crap**, . . . (Salinger 1945: 3)

The partially specified general extender (*and all that David Copperfield kind of crap*) downgrades this type of information, as well as the "more" that goes along with the standard routine for storytelling.

In [14], the speaker is downgrading another kind of social formula. In this excerpt, Diane Keaton is responding to an interviewer on the topic of what it's like to be an unmarried woman.

[14] I don't feel like I'm out there alone, exactly. Certainly
        when I was with men, I didn't feel buffered from every
        storm because I was with them. You can't get that from
        somebody else. I did not buy the fantasy of Prince
        Charming **and all that garbage**. (Collins 1995: 98)

Although she frequently encounters individuals who feel sorry for a woman (like herself) who isn't married, Keaton says she's doing just fine. In her experience, being with a man is not all it's cracked up to be. Keaton attributes low value to social scripts that create unrealistic expectations among women, saying, *I did not buy the fantasy of Prince Charming and all that garbage*. The downgrading general extender (*and all that garbage*) effectively signals that "there is more" and "it's worthless" and assumes "you know it is too." Used in this way, general extenders can have a strong rhetorical impact.

Excerpts [13]–[14] demonstrate how adjunctive general extenders can be used to downgrade routines against which the speaker or writer is rebelling. There are many other reasons a speaker may have for downgrading the "more," and these reasons vary according to context. As illustration, consider excerpts [15] and [16]. In [15], from an interview, Keith Richards, guitarist for the Rolling Stones, responds to the question "What's the worst part of getting old?"

[15] I haven't found it yet. I still zoom around and do what I do.
   I'd hate to have to go 'round thinking about [derisively]
   health **and shit like that**. (Heath 1997: 50)

Having acknowledged his extravagantly unhealthy lifestyle, including heavy drinking, smoking, experimentation with a variety of hard drugs, and sleep deprivation, Richards is delighted to be in such good physical shape. He says that *he'd hate to have to go 'round thinking about health and shit like that*. For Richards, having to think about health (and the "more" he'd have to think about if he were in bad shape) would alter his lifestyle in an extremely negative way. He uses the general extender *and shit like that* to ridicule that thought. This interpretation of Richards's utterance is also reflected in the interviewer's inserted comment [*derisively*].

In excerpt [16], from another interview, the singer Paula Cole is talking about how much work it was to produce her own album.

[16] I was on the phone 12 hours a day making budgets **and all that crap**. I know now that it's really the secretaries who do all the work. (*People*, 30 June, 1997)

For Cole, the organizational work that goes into producing an album (*making budgets and all that crap*) is tedious and boring. The general extender *and all that crap* downgrades the making of budgets and the "more" involved in this kind of work.

These last two examples, *health and shit like that* in [15] and *making budgets and all that crap* in [16], help to illustrate the way in which the speaker's attitude to the "more" can be incorporated as the speaker indicates awareness that there is indeed "more" to be said on the topics. We might also note the ironic effect achieved in *beautiful and shit* from the introductory quote of this chapter, partially repeated here as [17].

[17] you'll be there in the lights, all beautiful **an' shit**.

In this utterance, the speaker expresses some envy for the positive aspects of the woman's future success, but he reveals his negative attitude toward that success in the general extender. He acknowledges that there will be "more" to that success, but his feelings about it are not positive. There are other ways in which attitude to the "more" can be revealed in general extenders.

Reported Speech *and blah blah blah*

Adjunctive general extenders are frequently used in contemporary American English to downgrade the "more" that could have been said in reporting speech. For example, in [18], the speaker finds herself about to report material that she subsequently describes as *propaganda*. The "more" that might be said is downgraded to *and all that mess*.

[18] They kept sayin' y'know 'this isn't (*)'—**an' all
that mess**—I don't read all that propaganda . . .

A second example is presented in [19], in which a female speaker is reporting an incident involving a mutual acquaintance (Sue) and her mother. The two had been out shopping together, when Sue's mother suddenly collapsed on the sidewalk.

[19] Sue said she was walking along she heard this crash .
and didn't know what happened for a minute and looked
round and there was her mum on the ground behind her she
went to pick her up and . course her mother just cussed and
swore at her and said oh don't make such a bloody fuss sh .
everybody's looking **and all that nonsense**   (Cheepen and
Monaghan 1990: 150)

According to the speaker, rather than accepting Sue's offer of help to get back on her feet, Sue's mother *cussed and swore*, and said: *oh don't make such a bloody fuss sh . everybody's looking*. The speaker uses the general extender and *all that nonsense* to characterize what Sue's mother said (including the "more") as not worthy of further elaboration.

There is one adjunctive general extender that is becoming definitive in reporting speech (among familiars) for marking the "more" that might have been said as unimportant or having low value: *and blah blah blah*. Consider example [20], in which the speaker (Sara) is complaining about her employer, who she feels is being unreasonable. Sara was about to leave on vacation, and had asked her employer if she could pick up her paycheck a few days early.

[20] They don't wanna give me a paycheck today if I were to
      take a vacation next week they're like 'Wull, we'd hafta
      like—we'd hafta like mail it to you::: an' **blah blah blah**.'
      An' I'm like 'Hhhh! Nevermind.'

In her complaint, Sara reports what her employer said: *Wull, we'd hafta like—we'd hafta like mail it to you::: an' blah blah blah*. The general extender *an' blah blah blah* extends the utterance, indicating that there was more to this dispreferred and annoying response, but that the content of what was said is not significant for this hearer.

There are many variations on this form.[2] Two examples are shown in [21] and [22], where Donna is telling her best friend Blake about an argument she had with her husband, Henry. At this point in the interaction, Donna is reporting Henry's reaction to her complaint that he doesn't talk to her enough.

[21] Donna: He goes (.5) "Uh—You:: and Blake are really
      intelligent, and you can talk with him **an' dadada**, and I::
      can't do that." Or something. I mean this is his excuse for
      (.5) why we can't (.) I dunno be closer in terms of that kind
      of relationship.

[22] Donna: An' he's like "Wha::—" That's when the
      conversation came in—"Wull I can't do all the things he
      does an' I'm not your .hhh intellectual pee::r **bluh=bluh
      bluh=bluh**"

Donna is clearly frustrated by Henry's portrayal of himself as intellectually inferior and considers this a poor excuse for not talking to her. Donna uses the forms *an' dadada* and *bluh=bluh bluh=bluh* to downgrade the content of Henry's reported utterances and to indicate that there was more (of this nonsense) said. It may also be that, in Donna's assessment, the explicit mention of the "more" that is implicated by the adjunctive general extender would not only create an unnecessarily lengthy utterance; it might also obscure the message, by providing information irrelevant to the point she wants to make.

The general extender *(and) blah blah blah*, signaling "there is more, but it is irrelevant here," has certainly been adopted by advertisers. Example [23] is an advertisement for wine which relies on the downgrading effect of quadruple *blah* to make its point about ignoring conventional rules about wine.

[23] Red wine is for meat. White wine is for fish. *Blah! blah! blah! blah!* Forget the rules! Enjoy the wine.

Figure 9.3 provides another example. In figure 9.3, the bank advertisement describes the *blah* as "clouds of lingo" which is "tedious," and "intimidating," and the writer implies that such talk may "obscure a customer's understanding." Even though the bank considers the content of its message important, it acknowledges that recipients typically find the language it uses unclear and confusing.

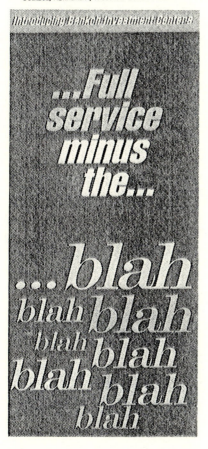

MUTUAL FUNDS • STOCKS • BONDS • ANNUITIES • IRAs
COLLEGE, RETIREMENT, TRUST AND ESTATE PLANNING

no blah *Full Service* to us means cutting through the clouds of lingo so common to our profession. Necessary, but tedious, fine print and intimidating terminology should never obscure a customer's understanding. It's our purpose to explain the complex in simple terms so clear-cut decisions can be made.

While there are many quality providers of investments, we offer the convenience of licensed investment professionals at a number of Bank of Hawaii branches statewide. Experienced investors will find the service refreshing. First timers who've never invested a dime beyond regular savings can expect meaningful answers to their questions. Stop by and ask us anything. Or call, 537-8500.

Bancorp Investment Group, Ltd.

Member NASD SIPC

Full Service plus... convenient Bank of Hawaii locations.

Investment products and services are not FDIC insured; are not deposits or other obligations or guaranteed by Bank of Hawaii or Bancorp Investment Group; and involve investment risks including possible loss of the principal amount invested. Bancorp Investment Group is a subsidiary of Bank of Hawaii.

Securities and investment products are sold through Bancorp Investment Group. Trust and estate planning services are sold through Hawaiian Trust Company.

Figure 9.3. Bank of Hawai'i ad.

This review of the range of forms being used as Quantity hedges, and the variety of contexts in which they occur, could be extended indefinitely. It seems that in contemporary discourse there is always "more" that could be said, but, for a number of reasons, there is no time or willingness to express it. I cannot pretend to know just what social factors are behind this phenomenon; however, by describing and illustrating some clear linguistic indicators, I have tried to provide one means of tracking and investigating its manifestation and future development.

PART FOUR

Conclusion

–10–

Summary

As soon as conversation is recorded on tape, it becomes a new entity—a taped conversation—that is different from the conversation as it occurred. For one thing, as has been pointed out, a recording is fixed in time and available for precise reproduction, whereas the very essence of talk is that it disappears as soon as it is uttered and can be imperfectly reconstructed, but not retrieved. In addition, the talk as uttered in the actual interaction is one channel of an integrated complex including nonverbal components such as facial expression, body movement, gesture, and so on.

Tannen (1984: 35)

These observations about studying talk should be kept in mind whenever we summarize the results of any investigation using conversational data. We are always studying fragments, and our analysis is always incomplete. And we often find that we have said very little about some instances of the phenomenon we have so carefully studied. For example, the role of the general extender *and so on* in this introductory quotation has not received much attention, nor have many other forms that are more typically found in written discourse. Bearing this cautionary note in mind, I will try to summarize some of the observations I have been able to make about my data.

In the preceding pages I have described and analyzed a set of linguistic forms which I have called "general extenders." General extenders are a class of expressions of the form conjunction plus noun phrase, which typically occur in clause-final position, are non-specific in reference, and extend otherwise grammatically complete utterances. These expressions can be divided into two basic types: adjunctive (those beginning with *and,* such as *and stuff like that, and everything*), and disjunctive (those beginning with *or,* such as *or anything, or something*).

In chapter 1, I identified some standard exemplars of this set of forms and illustrated their widespead distribution in many different genres. I noted that, although general extenders are found in both formal and informal contexts and in both spoken and written language, the frequency of these forms appears to be greatest in informal, spoken interaction among familiars. Next, I discussed the general approach and the type of data employed in this investigation. This discussion emphasized that the analysis would be based primarily on an examination of naturally occurring data within extended contexts, and that there is much in language that can be accounted for only in terms of a speaker–hearer context of occurrence.

The core of my analysis of general extenders was presented in chapters 2 through 9. The questions and issues addressed in these chapters were roughly divided into two major groups: those involving ideational function, and those involving interpersonal function.

In chapters 2 through 4, I explored the potential ideational function of general extenders. In chapter 2, I noted the widespead opinion that general extenders are examples of vague language. I then examined my data to investigate the proposal that general extenders function as list completers, focusing on assumptions tied to the role of social norms and expectations, particularly with regard to list construction. I found that, although certain examples might be viewed as support for the claim that general extenders function to complete three-part lists, general extenders occurred as third parts in less than one-fifth of the instances recorded. In the overwhelming majority of cases, general extenders occurred in structures with one item plus a general extender. I concluded that, from a linguistic perspective, the evidence from my data did not support a view of general extenders as predominantly being used to complete lists, or to mark an orientation to a norm of three-partedness.

In chapters 3 and 4, I focused on a mainly psycholinguistic approach, operating with the general assumption that general extenders could be analyzed in terms of reference to categories. I examined the proposal that general extenders combine with named exemplars, whose characteristics enable the hearer to identify a category the speaker has in mind. This involved an in-depth consideration of the current literature on category types and the conceptual organization of categories. I found that, while there is some evidence to support the claim that speakers can use general extenders in combination with named exemplars to indicate categories (chapter 3), it is implausible that speakers' and hearers' categories match in some objective way, or that a speaker's mention of a "prototypical" example will necessarily enable the hearer to infer the same set that the speaker has in mind (chapter 4). I demonstrated that the interpretation of general extenders is necessarily subjective, and that it is massively constrained by both linguistic and nonlinguistic context, as well as by background knowledge.

In chapters 5 through 9, I turned to a sociolinguistic perspective. I explored the role of general extenders as pragmatic expressions, focusing on the interpersonal function of these forms. This involved an analysis of how participants indicate shared knowledge and experience, and mark attitude toward the message and/or other participants. I found that, within their actual contexts of occurrence, general extenders appear to have a function that is primarily interpersonal and tied to the nature of the social relationship of the participants. In chapter 5, I explored how a speaker's use of a general extender invokes an assumption of intersubjectivity, thereby underscoring similarity and creating a sense of rapport. In chapter 6, I focused on the use of certain expressions (e.g., *or anything, or what, and all, and everything*) as intensifiers, to emphasize or highlight a preceding part of an utterance. In chapter 7, I demonstrated how a speaker's use of a general extender can reveal an orientation to politeness strategies. In chapters 8 and 9, I showed how a speaker's use of a general extender can be interpreted in terms of an orientation to expectations associated with the Gricean maxims of Quality and Quantity.

Interpersonal Functions of the Most Frequent Forms

As noted in chapter 3, the general consensus of previous studies has been that general extenders combine with named exemplars to implicate categories, and that based on the named exemplars, hearers are able to infer the category the speaker has in mind. Indeed, in almost all examples cited out of context, it is possible for the analyst to come up with a likely category as referent for a general extender. However, as demonstrated in chapters 5 through 9, within their actual contexts of occurrence, general extenders do not appear to be used with category implication as their most obvious function. When viewed in terms of their role within the interactive exchange of talk, general extenders appear to have a function that is primarily interpersonal and tied to the nature of the social relationships of the participants. Although a given form may serve more than one function, the context (both linguistic and nonlinguistic) of occurrence helps to constrain the interpretation on particular occasions of use.

A summary of the interpersonal functions associated with the most frequently occurring forms in my corpus is presented below.

Adjunctive General Extenders

and stuff

Typically indicates "more." Generally, the "more" need not be stated because the speaker assumes that the speaker and hearer share an intersubjective understanding which will enable the hearer to make sense of the speaker's message without further elaboration (in orientation to a constraint on cooperative interaction, such as the Gricean Maxim of Quantity). In some cases, the "more" can be treated as "not necessary" at the present time.

Also occurs as a marker of invited solidarity with the speaker as interactional partner (a strategy of positive politeness). In such cases, there may not be any discernible "more" to be understood.

and everything

Typically used as an intensifier, to emphasize or highlight a previous part of an assertion or question. Often used to express an evaluation of something as remarkable, surprising, or (a maximum) extreme.

It may also be used to indicate "more" which is assumed to be understood by the hearer (in orientation to a constraint on cooperative interaction, such as the Maxim of Quantity).

and blah blah blah

Typically indicates that more could be said. It is used to indicate that the "more" is "not necessary" to the hearer at the present time (in orientation to a constraint on cooperative interaction, such as the Maxim of Quantity). This particular general extender, and variations of it, are commonly found to occur in conjunction with reported speech that the speaker considers to be of little value.

Disjunctive General Extenders

or something

Typically used as a hedge to mark the content of an assertion as possibly inaccurate, or approximate (in orientation to a constraint on cooperative interaction, such as the Gricean Maxim of Quality). Commonly found to occur in conjunction with reported speech. Used in jokes, to mark a preceding part of an utterance as an exaggeration or analogy, which should not be taken literally.

Also found in invitations, offers, proposals, and requests, where it is used to indicate alternative options, and to express tentativeness (a strategy of negative politeness).

or anything

Typically used as an intensifier, to emphasize or highlight a previous part of an assertion or question. Often used to express an evaluation of something as surprising, or (a minimum) extreme.

Also found in invitations, offers, proposals, and requests, where it is used to indicate alternative options (a strategy of negative politeness).

or whatever

Typically used as a hedge to mark the content of an assertion as possibly inaccurate (in orientation to a constraint on cooperative interaction, such as the Maxim of Quality). Also conveys an attitude that, from the speaker's perspective, the accuracy is unimportant. On some occasions, may convey a stronger, dismissive attitude of "I don't care."

Also occurs in invitations, offers, proposals, and requests, where it is used to indicate a lack of commitment to a stated option and a willingness to consider alternatives (a strategy of negative politeness).

From these descriptions, we can note that the two most common forms (*and stuff, or something*) can be characterized interpersonally along two distinct dimensions. The adjunctive general extender *and stuff* signals both "I'm in danger of not saying enough" and "we are close and you know what I mean." The disjunctive general extender *or something* signals both "I'm in danger of not being strictly accurate" and "there may be an alternative and you know what I mean."

Multifunctionality

Throughout the preceding chapters, I have attempted to isolate the different possible functions of general extenders and to provide good illustrations of each separate function, as if the forms had single functions on each occasion of use. The advantage of this analytic convenience with regard to the identification of separate functions is offset by a serious drawback in terms of recognizing the multifunctionality of many of these forms on particular occasions of use. Having pulled apart many of those functional strands in order to look at them more closely, I would now like to look at how those distinct strands can be combined in the rich texture of a single instance.

Using example [1], I will discuss several aspects of the contextualized use of one example of the most common adjunctive general extender. Using example [2], I will look at several elements involved in the contextualized use of an example of the most common disjunctive general extender.

An' stuff

Previously considered very briefly in chapter 2, example [1] is uttered by Rosie when she is making a proposal to her friend Julie about how they will organize their return from a hiking/camping trip in a wilderness area. She is suggesting that they make the long hike back together.

[1]   Rosie: We'll get an early start, an' I was thinking if we
         wanted to bring in the coo::ler, we could, an' have it—each
         pitch in a little bit of money an' have Mike take it out by
         boat. So that we can put all the kitchen stuff in the::re, an'
         all the heavy stuff, an' just pack out our clo::thes an' tents
         an' stuff.

As I have emphasized at several points, the most fundamental element in the use of *and stuff* is "there is more." In the particular case of *an' stuff* in [1], we can take several analytic perspectives on how the "more" is to be interpreted:

(1) Viewed as a three-part list, the final part of example [1] (*our clo::thes an' tents an' stuff*) would simply be interpreted as indicating that there are "more" items in that list that the speaker has in mind. Following the pattern established by the first two exemplars, we could imagine some other items in such a list. We would also be required to recognize that there is no way of knowing whether the items listed by an analyst would match those that the speaker had in mind on that occasion.

(2) In terms of reference, the "more" items could be identified as not simply isolated elements in a list, but connected elements belonging to a certain category. Known members of that category are *clothes* and *tents*, which are unlikely to lead to the identification of a standard lexicalized category label. Using other contextual clues in [1], we might construct an ad hoc category such as "other light items used during a hiking and camping trip." Once again, however, the analyst's selection of other members of such a category cannot be treated as identical to what the speaker had in mind on that occasion.

(3) On more careful consideration, we must recognize that the actual ad hoc category implicated by *an' stuff* in [1] can be reconstructed only under an assumption of intersubjectivity, which might be represented as "there is more and you know what I mean." Given this assumption, it is not actually necessary that a particular category or other items from that category would have to be instantiated in any way. Viewed intersubjectively, the potential category becomes even less amenable to reconstruction by the analyst, objectively and independently, because it would depend on the shared knowledge and experience of these conversational familiars.

(4) By using this marker of intersubjectivity (*an' stuff*), similar in many ways to *you know*, the speaker is indicating positive politeness and appealing to solidarity in a common goal, as she makes a proposal about a future activity involving both speakers. There is a potential imposition of one speaker's expressed plans on the behavior of another, and the face-threatening impact of that imposition is being averted in advance by a strategy of positive politeness based on shared experience and a common goal. The non-specific nature of the "more" involved at this stage allows both participants to treat the goal as shared, even if the eventual details involved in *an' stuff* might be different.

(5) Simultaneously, the speaker's use of the intersubjective marker (*an' stuff*) signals this cooperative conversational partner's orientation to expectations that she will say neither too much nor too little in organizing her communicative message. She is operating within the constraints of the Gricean Maxim of Quantity, signaling

"there is more and you know what I mean, so I don't have do be more explicit at this point."

There are, no doubt, other subtle dimensions to what is being accomplished by the general extender (*an' stuff*) on this occasion, but the preceding five observations provide some support for a claim of richly textured multifunctionality.

Or something like that

Example [2] is from a telephone conversation between Jim and his sister Mary. Mary is about to move out of her apartment, and in a previous conversation she had offered to give some of her furniture to Jim.

[2] 1. Jim: When are you leavin'?
2. Mary: The eleventh.
3. Jim: Whoa, quick.
4. Mary: Yeah.
5. Jim: Nine day—a week an' a half.
6. Mary: Yeah. We're gonna probably go over to mom and dad's on Sunday night, but (.) um (.5) I don't know. We have a lotta things we have to do before we leave, so: // every day's gettin' full
7. Jim: (*) (.) Am I still pickin' up a dre:sser **or something like that**?
8. Mary: Yea:h.
9. Jim: Okay.
10. Mary: U://m
11. Jim: Lemme know when that's happening.

At this point, I would like to consider some of the different analytic perspectives that might be taken on how the disjunctive general extender *or something like that* in turn 7 is to be interpreted.

(1) The most literal interpretation of a disjunctive general extender is that there is an "alternative." By using *or something like that* in [2], Jim is indicating that there is a possible alternative to what he states prior to the general extender. Objectively, we do not know if that is an alternative to an action (*picking up*) or to an entity (*a dresser*) or even to the whole event.

(2) From the perspective of reference, we can view the named exemplar (*a dresser*) as a member of a certain category that will also include a possible alternative. The most obvious lexicalized category here is "furniture," but there is no other evidence in this particular interaction to provide independent support for choosing this category. From the categorization perspective, we might propose that *or*

something like that is implicating, as a default, some member of the category "furniture."

(3) From the response by Mary, immediately following *or something like that*, we have interactive evidence that what Jim has said is not completely mistaken. Mary's response (*Yeah*) confirms that Jim's description has been intersubjectively effective. From the perspective of intersubjectivity, Jim's use of *or something like that* can be seen as "there is a possible alternative, but you know what I mean." In this case, the intersubjective interpretation appears to be supported for both speakers by what had been said in a previous conversation.

(4) The general extender in this case is placed at the end of a question about a possible future event. Jim is asking about what he will be doing rather than stating that he will do it. There is a clear danger of imposition-on-other involved in this possible event, because the item of furniture belongs to the (very busy) other. By asking about the event and concluding with *or something like that*, Jim is indicating negative politeness in terms of avoiding imposition and expressing the possibility of an alternative. As he introduces the topic of his *picking up a dre:sser*, Jim is marking his awareness of the face-threatening impact of the potential imposition involved and attempting to avert it in advance. The non-specific nature of the clause-final expression *or something like that* allows for an alternative, and for the interlocutor to restate the nature of the action or the entity involved.

(5) As part of his face-saving move in [2], Jim's question can also be seen in terms of an orientation to expectations associated with the Maxim of Quality. It is possible that he is mistaken about what is going to happen, or about what the item of furniture is appropriately called. As a hedge on expectations of accuracy, Jim attaches the disjunctive general extender (*or something like that*) to his proposal (*picking up a dresser*) and thereby signals "I believe this is what is going to happen, but I may be mistaken and there may be an alternative, but you and I know what I mean."

Other subtle implications could, I am sure, be revealed by further consideration of how this general extender (*or something like that*) was used on this occasion, but these five observations begin to provide a sense of how richly textured the multifunctionality of these forms can be within interactive discourse.

What My Aunt Was Saying

Returning to the utterance that I quoted at the beginning of this investigation, we are now in a better position to analyze what my aunt's message was when she said, *Did you wanna go look at some shoes and stuff, or something, or what?* In using *and stuff*, my aunt was indicating that *shoes* (which we had already talked about) were just one example of the things we could look at in the shopping mall, and she was marking an assumption that, since we shared common knowlege of what else is found in a shopping mall, she didn't have to mention anything else explicitly. The expression *or something* added an element of negative politeness, signalling that to *look at some shoes and stuff* was just one of the things we might do that afternoon, and that she was willing to entertain other possibilities. The final *or what* emphasized her desire to get a response and urged me to express an opinion. Far from being vague expressions or empty fillers, these general extenders are crucial markers of interpersonal talk. This survey of some of their more obvious uses will, I hope, encourage others to analyze these forms more closely, to discover other possible functions, to investigate equivalent forms in other languages, *and so on.*

Notes

Chapter 1

1. Eric Kellerman has drawn my attention to a student thesis (Graman 1998) on the *Catcher in the Rye* in which 635 general extenders were counted, representing an average of more than three per page. It is worth emphasizing that this novel was first published almost fifty years ago, so these forms cannot be treated as new or ephemeral creations of the current generation.

2. On a wide range of features, spoken language has been shown to differ from written language (see Biber 1991, Brown and Yule 1983b, Halliday 1989, Horowitz and Samuels 1987, Tannen 1982). The observation that general extenders occur more frequently in spoken contexts is supported by the studies of Ball and Ariel (1978), DuBois (1993) and Ediger (1995). It should be emphasized that my study focuses on the use of spoken language; no substantive claims will be made with regard to the use of general extenders in written discourse.

3. It seems reasonable to assume that general extenders occur in most languages, though perhaps not with similar functions. Moreover, there may already exist studies of these forms in other languages. Yumiko Ohara has informed me that Endo and Yabe (1996) and Honda (1996) examine the use of some general extenders in Japanese.

4. An embedded S is frequently analyzed under an NP node, with reported speech as a well-known case (e.g., Bicky said, "It's syntax. Don't think about it, just do it," *or something like that*).

5. Surprisingly, there has been relatively little previous research on these forms. Among those who have looked at some of the forms are Aijmer (1985), Ball and Ariel (1978), Channell (1994), Dines (1980), DuBois (1993), Jefferson (1990), and Ward and Birner (1993). Although general extenders are not the main focus of study in Romaine and Lange (1991), Lerner (1994), or Macaulay (1985, 1991), these works contain brief discussions of some forms. Terms used to denote these forms have included "set-marking tags" (Dines 1980, Ward and Birner 1993), "generalized list completers" (Jefferson 1990, Lerner 1994), "extension particles" (DuBois 1993), and "vague category identifiers" (Channell 1994).

6. While the analysis of nonverbal behavior and paralinguistic features would undoubtedly add to our knowledge of how general extenders are used, a consideration of these particular factors lies beyond the scope of this study.

7. I am a participant in some of the telephone conversations. Although the involvement of the analyst as an occasional participant/observer might be considered a disadvantage in some theoretical frameworks, I believe that this was not the case in the current investigation. My involvement in this capacity, and my familiarity with the situations discussed, allowed me to better understand how relevant expressions were being used by these participants on the specific occasions recorded (see Tannen 1984 for similar arguments).

Chapter 2

1. The socio-cultural notion of three-partedness may have a strong connection to the Western European, Christian concept of the Trinity (Father, Son, and Holy Ghost). For a discussion of "threes" in our culture, see Scollon and Scollon (1981: 33ff). For more on lists, see Schiffrin (1994b).

2. This issue will be explored later in chapter 4, in terms of what Lyons (1977) called first-, second-, and third-order entities. As noted in chapter 1, the fact that general extenders are not constrained by strict grammatical agreement requirements contributes to the difficulty of determining which element(s) a general extender is coordinated with.

Chapter 3

1. It lies beyond the scope of this work to give a comprehensive account of theories of categorization, or to present a critical evaluation of such theories. This preliminary discussion is presented in an effort to elucidate aspects of theories of categorization that will be relevant to the study at hand. For more comprehensive treatments of categorization, see Barsalou (1992), G. Lakoff (1987a), Neisser (1987), Taylor (1995), and van Mechelen et al. (1993).

2. It appears that much of this discussion was presaged in Wittgenstein's work, particularly with regard to the notions of "paradigm examples" and "language games" (see Bloor 1983). A point of interest with regard to the notion of category boundaries is that "categories tend to be viewed as being separate from each other and as clear-cut as possible" (Rosch 1978: 35). Whereas the classical view of categories "achieves this by means of necessary and sufficient conditions for category membership," the contemporary view achieves this sense of "separateness and clarity of actually continuous categories by conceiving of each in terms of its clear cases, rather than its boundaries" (Rosch 1978: 35–36).

3. Berlin suggests that ethnobiological classification is one area that is "rather precisely defined," in that "there are fairly well agreed upon procedures for recognizing an instance of some particular plant or animal type that are less ambiguous than recognizing instances of demons, mythical beings, binary oppositions, or, for that matter, even making judgements of grammaticality" (1978: 9). However, those who embrace the contemporary notion of category ultimately believe that the conception of biological species as natural kinds

which are defined by common essential properties is inaccurate, and that it will be left behind (see G. Lakoff 1987a).

4. One form that is not easily interpreted as category implicative is *and blah blah blah*. Special attention will be given to this form in chapter 9.

5. Where lexicalized categories represent things in the environment, they often reflect its correlational structure and form more salient groups of entities. Barsalou defines the correlational structure of the environment as "properties of entities in the environment that are not independent but, instead, form clusters of correlated properties. For example, if an entity has feathers, there is a much higher probability that it flies and builds nests, than that it swims and has gills" (1983: 214).

6. For a more detailed discussion of locally contingent categorization in discourse, see Overstreet and Yule (1997a).

Chapter 4

1. Channell's (1994) research was designed to force respondents to treat general extenders as forms that are used instead of naming other items. Her results actually demonstrate that, when forced to do so, respondents will give an extremely large and diverse set of items that the speaker might have had in mind when using a noun phrase containing a general extender. The actual results provide little support either for a prototype-based analysis or for one based on category implication. They simply show that, in an experimental setting, respondents can demonstrate an extremely large number of associations between words.

2. One way to talk about this is in terms of target and contrast categories. See Bateson (1955), who writes of a "proper ground" for a class, and Bilmes (1985), for a discussion of this concept.

3. It is, of course, impossible for a speaker to spell out everything she wishes to convey in a message. Yet, as Ziff (1972: 131–139) has noted, the lack of specification doesn't usually cause a problem for hearers. This is true because speakers and hearers share conceptual schemes, and speakers appeal to what is ordinary, common, or typical in these schemes when they employ a particular form of representation.

4. My translation from the German.

Chapter 5

1. My translation from the German.

Chapter 6

1. In this section I am using the concept of a formulaic construction, rather than the more generally recognized formulaic language which is based on specific lexical items or phrases. As Coulmas (1981) has noted, the use of formulas

and routines is a way of indicating assumptions of familiarity and affirming social relationships. For more on this topic, see Fillmore, Kay, and O'Connor (1988), Hakuta (1974), Kay (1997), Nattinger and DeCarrico (1992), Pawley and Syder (1983), and Wong Fillmore (1994). For more on disclaimers and aspects of alignment talk, see Buttny (1993), Goffman (1971), Hall and Hewitt (1970), Hewitt and Hall (1973), Scott and Lyman (1968), and Schegloff, Jefferson, and Sacks (1977).

2. Haiman has noted that the general extender *or anything* commonly occurs in the structure *Not that X or anything*, where it appears to emphasize the "belittling constituent" *not that*, but in fact is used to mock it. E.g., "*Not that you annoyed me or anything* (=You annoyed the hell out of me)" (1998: 55).

Chapter 8

1. Epistemic modals are used to indicate deductions or conclusions by the speaker (or writer). For more on epistemic modality, see Palmer (1986) and Yule (1998).

2. Note that in [12], *like* precedes the quoted material. This also marks it as just one of a number of possible utterances, similar in form and content, that could have been said. According to Romaine and Lange (1991), *like* may be used to "evoke examples of what might have been said/thought or might be said/thought either on particular or repeated occasions in the past or in hypothetical instances in the future" (1991: 247).

Chapter 9

1. As a number of writers have pointed out (e.g., Horn 1984, Levinson 1983, Sperber and Wilson 1995), the four Gricean maxims are not mutually exclusive. Although I will not discuss the maxims of Relation and Manner, there is little doubt that any hedge on Quantity will also be tied, in some respect, to the expectations of relevance, clarity, and brevity on its particular occasion of use.

2. On the popular American television show *Seinfeld*, the form *(and) yada yada yada* seems to function as a variation on the form *(and) blah blah blah*, to indicate "there is more, but the details are irrelevant here." In one episode, the show's characters discuss at length the possibility that speakers may use *(and) yada yada yada* to avoid providing (incriminating) details about the "more" that it indicates.

References

Aijmer, Karin. 1985. "What Happens at the End of Our Utterances?—
The Use of Utterance-Final Tags Introduced by 'and' and 'or.'" *Papers from the 8th Scandinavian Conference of Linguistics*, 366–389. Copenhagen: Institut for Philologie, Kopenhaven University.

Albee, Edward. 1962. *Who's Afraid of Virginia Woolf?* New York: Atheneum.

Allwood, Jens, Lars-Gunnar Andersson, and Östen Dahl. 1977. *Logic in Linguistics*. Cambridge: Cambridge University Press.

Ariel, Mira. 1994. "Pragmatic Operators." In *Encyclopedia of Languages and Linguistics*, edited by R. E. Asher, 6: 3250–3253. Oxford: Pergamon and Aberdeen University Press.

Atkinson, John, and John Heritage, eds. 1984. *Structures of Social Action*. Cambridge: Cambridge University Press.

Austen, Jane. 1818/1961. *Persuasion*. London: The Folio Society.

Baker, Charlotte. 1975. "'This Is Just a First Approximation, but. . .'" *Papers from the Eleventh Regional Meeting*, 37–47. Chicago: Chicago Linguistic Society.

Ball, Catherine, and Mira Ariel. 1978. "Or Something, etc." In *Penn Review of Linguistics*, edited by C. Ball and L. Matossian, 3: 35–45. Department of Linguistics, University of Pennsylvania.

Barsalou, Lawrence. 1983. "Ad hoc categories." *Memory and Cognition* 11: 211–227.

——. 1987. "The Instability of Graded Structure: Implications for the Nature of Concepts." In *Concepts and Conceptual Development*, edited by U. Neisser, 101–140. Cambridge: Cambridge University Press.

——. 1992. *Cognitive Psychology*. Hillsdale, N. J.: Lawrence Erlbaum.

Bartlett, Frederick C. 1932. *Remembering*. Cambridge: Cambridge University Press.

Bateson, Gregory. 1955. "The Message 'This is Play.'" In *Group Processes: Transactions of the Second Conference*, edited by B. Schaffner, 145-242. Madison, N. J.: Madison Printing Company.

Bell, Robert, Christopher Zahn, and Robert Hopper. 1984. "Disclaiming: A Test of Two Competing Views." *Communication Quarterly* 32: 28–36.

Berlin, Brent. 1978. "Ethnobiological Classification." In *Cognition and Categorization*, edited by E. Rosch and B. Lloyd, 9–26. Hillsdale, N. J.: Lawrence Erlbaum.

Berlin, Brent, D. E. Breedlove, and P. H. Raven. 1968. "Covert Categories and Folk Taxonomies." *American Anthropologist* 70: 290–299.

Biber, Douglas. 1991. *Variation Across Speech and Writing*. Cambridge: Cambridge University Press.

Bickerton, Derek. 1981. *Roots of Language*. Ann Arbor, Mich.: Karoma.

Bilmes, Jack. 1982. "The Joke's on You, Goldilocks: A Reinterpretation of The Three Bears." *Semiotica* 39: 269–283.

———. 1985. "'Why that Now?' Two Kinds of Conversational Meaning." *Discourse Processes* 8: 319–355.

———. 1986. *Discourse and Behavior*. New York: Plenum.

———. 1988. "Category and Rule in Conversation Analysis." *International Pragmatics Association, Papers in Pragmatics* 2: 25–59.

Bloor, David. 1983. *Wittgenstein: A Social Theory of Knowledge*. New York: Columbia University Press.

Brown, Gillian, and George Yule. 1983a. *Discourse Analysis*. Cambridge: Cambridge University Press.

———. 1983b. *Teaching the Spoken Language*. Cambridge: Cambridge University Press.

Brown, Penelope, and Stephen Levinson. 1987. *Politeness*. Cambridge: Cambridge University Press.

Bruner, Jerome, Jacqueline Goodnow, and George Austin. 1956. *A Study of Thinking*. New York: John Wiley and Sons.

Buttny, Richard. 1993. *Social Accountability in Communication*. London: Sage.

Carnap, Rudolf. 1947. *Meaning and Necessity*. Chicago: University of Chicago Press.

———. 1959. *The Logical Syntax of Language*. Patterson, N. J.: Littlefield, Adams.

Channell, Joanna. 1994. *Vague Language*. Oxford: Oxford University Press.

Cheepen, Christine, and James Monaghan. 1990. *Spoken English: A Practical Guide*. London: Pinter.

Chi, M., P. Feltovich, and R. Glaser. 1981. "Categorization and Representation of Physics Problems by Experts and Novices." *Cognitive Science* 5: 121–152.

Chomsky, Noam. 1957. *Syntactic Structures*. The Hague: Mouton.

———. 1966. *Cartesian Linguistics*. New York: Harper and Row.

———. 1968. *Language and Mind*. New York: Harcourt, Brace and World.

Cicourel, Aaron. 1974. *Cognitive Sociology*. New York: Free Press.

Clark, Herbert, and Deanna Wilkes–Gibbs. 1986. "Referring as a Collaborative Process." *Cognition* 22: 1–39.

Codrescu, Andrei. 1994. *Zombification*. New York: St. Martin's.

Collins, Nancy. 1995. "Annie Hall Doesn't Live Here Anymore." *Vanity Fair*, Nov. 92–98.

Coulmas, Florian. 1981. *Conversational Routine*. The Hague: Mouton.

Craig, Robert, and Karen Tracy, eds. 1983. *Conversational Coherence: Form, Structure, and Strategy*. Beverly Hills, Calif.: Sage.

Cruse, D. A. 1986. *Lexical Semantics*. Cambridge: Cambridge University Press.

Davidson, Judy. 1984. "Subsequent Versions of Invitations, Offers, Requests, and Proposals Dealing with Potential or Actual Rejection." In *Stuctures of Social Action*, edited by J. Atkinson, and J. Heritage, 102–128. Cambridge: Cambridge University Press.

Dines, Elizabeth. 1980. "Variation in Discourse—and stuff like that." *Language in Society* 1: 13–31.

Dougherty, J. W. D. 1981. "Salience and Relativity in Classification." In *Language, Culture and Cognition: Anthropological Perspectives*, edited by Ronald Casson, 163–180. New York: Macmillan.

DuBois, Sylvie. 1993. "Extension particles, etc." *Language Variation and Change* 4: 179–203.

Dunne, Dominick. 1997. *Another City, Not My Own*. New York: Crown.

Durkheim, Emile. 1915. *The Elementary Forms of Religious Life*. London: George Allen & Unwin.

Ediger, Anne. 1995. *An Analysis of Set–marking Tags in the English Language*. Dissertation, University of California, Los Angeles.

Endo, O., and H. Yabe. 1996. "Hanashi kotoba ni tokuchootekina go no atarashii yoohoo to sedaisa." [New usages and age differences in spoken language] *Kotoba* 16: 114–127.

Ephron, Nora. *Heartburn*. 1983. New York: Random House.

Fillmore, Charles, Paul Kay, and Mary O'Connor. 1988. "Regularity and Idiomaticity in Grammatical Constructions: The Case of *Let Alone*." *Language* 64: 501–538.

Fisher, Carrie. 1987. *Postcards from the Edge*. New York: Simon and Schuster.

Frake, Charles. 1969. "The Ethnographic Study of Cognitive Systems." In *Cognitive Anthropology*, edited by S. Tyler, 28–40. New York: Holt, Rinehart and Winston.

Garfinkel, Harold. 1963. "A Conception of, and Experiments with 'Trust' as a Condition of Stable Concerted Actions." In *Motivation and Social Interaction*, edited by O. J. Harvey, 187–238. New York: Ronald Press.

——. 1967. *Studies in Ethnomethodology*. Englewood Cliffs, N. J.: Prentice-Hall.

Gelman, Susan, J. D. Coley, and G. M. Gottfried. 1994. "Essential Beliefs in Children: The Acquisition of Concepts and Theories." In *Mapping the Mind: Domain Specificity in Cognition and Culture*, edited by L. A. Hirschfeld and S. A. Gelman, 346–365. New York: Cambridge University Press.

Givón, Talmy. 1984. *Syntax: A Functional-Typological Introduction*. Amsterdam: John Benjamins.

Gliedman, John. 1983. "Interview: Noam Chomsky." *Omni*, Nov. 113–116, 171–174.

Goffman, Erving. 1959. *The Presentation of Self in Everyday Life*. New York: Doubleday.

——. 1967. *Interaction Ritual: Essays on Face–to–Face Behavior*. New York: Doubleday Anchor.

——. 1971. *Relations in Public*. London: Allen Lane.

Goodman, N. 1972. "Seven Strictures on Similarity." In *Problems and Projects*, edited by N. Goodman, 437–447. Indianapolis, Ind: Bobbs Merrill.

Grace, George. 1987. *The Linguistic Construction of Reality*. London: Croom Helm.

Graman, Patrick. 1998. *General Extenders in English and Dutch: A Comparison of The Catcher in the Rye and Three Translations*. Thesis, Department of English, Katholieke Universiteit, Nijmegen.

Grice, H. Paul. 1975. "Logic and Conversation." In *Syntax and Semantics 3: Speech Acts*, edited by P. Cole and J. Morgan, 41–58. New York: Academic Press.

Gumperz, John. 1984. "Communicative Competence Revisited." In *Meaning, Form and Use in Context: Linguistic Applications*, edited by D. Schiffrin, 278–289. Washington, D.C.: Georgetown University Press.

Guthrie, Anna. 1994. *Quotative Tense Shift in American English Authority-Encounter Narratives*. Master's thesis, University of California, San Bernardino.

Haiman, John. 1980. "The Iconicity of Grammar: Isomorphism and Motivation." *Language* 56: 515–540.

———. 1983. "Iconic and Economic Motivation." *Language* 59: 781–819.

———. 1998. *Talk is Cheap*. Oxford: Oxford University Press.

Hakuta, Kenji. 1974. "Prefabricated Patterns and the Emergence of Structure in Second Language Acquisition." *Language Learning* 24: 287–297.

Hall, Peter, and John Hewitt. 1970. "The Quasi–Theory of Communication and the Management of Dissent." *Social Problems* 18: 17–27.

Halliday, Michael A. K. 1970. "Language Structure and Language Function." In *New Horizons in Linguistics*, edited by John Lyons, 140–165. U. K.: Penguin.

———. 1989. *Spoken and Written Language*. Oxford: Oxford University Press.

Hatch, Evelyn. 1992. *Discourse and Language Education*. Cambridge: Cambridge University Press.

Have, Paul ten. 1991. "Talk and Institution: A Reconsideration of the 'Asymmetry' of Doctor–Patient Interaction." In *Talk and Social Structure: Studies in Ethnomethodology and Conversation Analysis*, edited by D. Boden, and D. H. Zimmerman, 138–163. Cambridge: Polity.

Heath, Chris. 1997. "On the Road with the Rolling Stones." *Rolling Stone*, Dec., 50–53, 88–90.

Heritage, John. 1984. *Garfinkel and Ethnomethodology*. Cambridge: Polity.

Hewitt John, and Peter Hall. 1973. "Social Problems, Problematic Situations, and Quasi-Theories." *American Sociological Review* 38: 367–374.

Hewitt, John, and Randall Stokes. 1975. "Disclaimers." *American Sociological Review* 40: 1–11.

Honda, Akiko. 1996. "Daigaku koogi ni okeru kotoba no danjosa." [Gender differences in language use in university lectures] *Kotoba* 16: 15.

Horn, Laurence. 1984. "Toward a New Taxonomy for Pragmatic Inference: Q–Based and R–Based Implicature." In *Meaning, Form and Use in Context: Linguistic Applications*, edited by D. Schiffrin, 11–42. Washington, D. C.: Georgetown University Press.

Horowitz, Rosalind, and S. J. Samuels, eds. 1987. *Comprehending Oral and Written Language*. Orlando, Fla.: Academic Press.

Husserl, Edmund. 1929/1977. *Formale und tranzendentale Logik*. The Hague: Martinus Nijhoff.

Jackendoff, Ray. 1985. *Semantics and Cognition*. Cambridge, Mass.: MIT Press.

Jefferson, Gail. 1990. "List-Construction as a Task and Resource." In *Interaction Competence,* edited by George Psathas, 63–92. Lanham, Md.: University Press of America.

Kasper, Gabriele. 1994. "Politeness." In *Encyclopedia of Languages and Linguistics,* edited by R. E. Asher, 6: 3206–11. Oxford: Pergamon and Aberdeen University Press.

Kay, Paul. 1997. *Words and the Grammar of Context.* Stanford, Calif.: CSLI Publications.

Keil, F. C. 1991. "Theories, Concepts, and the Acquisition of Word Meaning." In *Perspectives on Language and Thought: Interrelations in Development,* edited by S. A. Gelman and J. P. Byrnes, 197–221. New York: Cambridge University Press.

Kirsner, Robert. 1985. "Iconicity and Grammatical Meaning." In *Iconicity in Syntax,* edited by John Haiman, 249–264. Amsterdam and Philadelphia: John Benjamins.

Koike, Dale. 1996. "Functions of the Adverbial *ya* in Spanish Narrative Discourse." *Journal of Pragmatics* 25: 267–279.

Krauss, Robert. 1987. "The Role of the Listener: Addressee Influences on Message Formulation." *Language and Social Psychology* 6: 81–97.

Krauss, Robert, and Sam Glucksberg. 1977. "Social and Nonsocial Speech." *Scientific American* 236: 100–105.

Labov, William. 1973. "The Boundaries of Words and their Meanings." In *New Ways of Analyzing Variation in English,* edited by C. J. N. Bailey and R. W. Shuy; 340–373. Washington, D. C.: Georgetown University Press.

Lakoff, George. 1972. "Hedges: A Study in Meaning Criteria and the Logic of Fuzzy Concepts." In *Papers from the Eighth RegionalMeeting of the Chicago Linguistic Society.* Also in *Journal of Philosophical Logic* 2 (1973): 458–508.

———. 1987a. *Women, Fire, and Dangerous Things.* Chicago: University of Chicago Press.

———. 1987b. "Cognitive Models and Prototype Theory." In *Concepts and Conceptual Development,* edited by U. Neisser, 63–100. Cambridge: Cambridge University Press.

———. 1995. "Embodied Minds and Meanings." In *Speaking Minds: Interviews with Twenty Eminent Cognitive Scientists,* edited by P. Baumgartner and S. Payr, 115–130. Princeton, N. J.: Princeton University Press.

Lakoff, Robin. 1973. "The Logic of Politeness; Or, Minding Your P's and Q's." *Papers from the 9th Regional Meeting of the Chicago Linguistic Society,* 292–305. Chicago: University of Chicago Press.

———. 1990. *Talking Power.* New York: Basic Books.

Landon, M. 1944. *Anna and the King of Siam.* New York: John Day.

Lee, K. C. 1998. "Environment is GNP." *Chosun-Ilbo* [Korean daily newspaper], Oct. 15: 28.

Lerner, Gene. 1994. "Responsive List Construction." *Language and Social Psychology* 13: 20–33.

Levinson, Stephen. 1983. *Pragmatics.* Cambridge: Cambridge University Press.

———. 1987. "Minimization and Conversational Inference." In *The Pragmatic Perspective: Selected Papers from the 1985 International Pragmatics Conference,* 61–129. Amsterdam: John Benjamins.

Lounsbury, Floyd. 1964. "A Formal Account of the Crow- and Omaha-Type Kinship Terminologies." In *Explorations in Cultural Anthropology,* edited by W. H. Goodenough, 351–394. New York: McGraw-Hill. Reprinted in *Cognitive Anthropology,* edited by Stephen A. Tyler, 212–254. New York: Holt, Rinehart, and Winston.

Lyons, John. 1977. *Semantics.* Cambridge: Cambridge University Press.

Macaulay, Ronald. 1985. "The Narrative Skills of a Scottish Coal Miner." In *Focus On: Scotland,* edited by Manfred Görlach, 101–124. Amsterdam: John Benjamins.

––––. 1991. *Locating Dialect in Discourse.* Oxford: Oxford University Press.

Martinet, A. 1962. *A Functional View of Language.* Oxford: Clarendon Press.

Mathis, Terrie. 1992. *The Form and Function of Constructed Dialogue in Reported Speech.* Dissertation, Louisiana State University.

Mathis, Terrie, and George Yule. 1994. "Zero Quotatives." *Discourse Processes* 18: 63–76.

McLaughlin, Margaret. 1984. *Conversation: How Talk Is Organized.* Beverly Hills, Calif.: Sage.

McGuire, James. 1938. *He Moolelo Pokole.* Honolulu: Collegiate Press.

Mead, George H. 1938. *Philosophy of the Act.* Chicago: University of Chicago Press.

Medin, Douglas. 1989. "Concepts and Conceptual Structure." *American Psychologist* 44: 1469–81.

Medin, Douglas, and Edward E. Smith. 1984. "Concepts and Concept Formation." *Annual Review of Psychology* 35: 113–38.

Medin, Douglas, and William Wattenmaker. 1987. "Category Cohesiveness, Theories, and Cognitive Archeology." In *Concepts and Conceptual Development,* edited by U. Neisser, 25–62. Cambridge: Cambridge University Press.

Mervis, C. B., and Eleanor Rosch. 1981. "Categorization of Natural Objects." *Annual Review of Psychology* 32: 89–115.

Mey, Jacob L. 1993. *Pragmatics.* Oxford: Blackwell.

Miller, George. 1978. "Practical and Lexical Knowledge." In *Cognition and Categorization,* edited by E. Rosch and B. Lloyd, 305–319. Hillsdale, N. J.: Lawrence Erlbaum.

Minsky, Marvin. 1975. "A Framework for Representing Knowledge." In *The Psychology of Computer Vision,* edited by P. H. Winston. New York: McGraw–Hill.

Murphy, Gregory. 1993. "Theories and Concept Formation." In *Categories and Concepts,* edited by I. van Mechelen et al. 173–200. London: Academic Press.

Murphy, Gregory, and Douglas Medin. 1985. "The Role of Theories in Conceptual Coherence." *Psychological Review* 92: 289–316.

Murphy, Gregory, and L. Wright. 1984. "Changes in Conceptual Structure with Expertise: Differences Between Real-World Experts and Novices." *Journal of Experimental Psychology: Learning, Memory, and Cognition* 10: 144–155.

Nattinger, James, and Jeanette DeCarrico. 1992. *Lexical Phrases and Language Teaching.* Oxford: Oxford University Press.

Neisser, Ulrich, ed. 1987. *Concepts and Conceptual Development.* Cambridge: Cambridge University Press.

Nelson, Katherine. 1983. "The Derivation of Concepts and Categories from Event Representations." In *New Trends in Conceptual Representation: Challenges to Piaget's Theory?*, edited by Ellin Scholnick, 129-149. N. J.: Lawrence Erlbaum.

Oden, G. C. 1987. "Concept, Knowledge, Thought." *Annual Review of Psychology* 38: 203–227.

Östman, Jan-Ola. 1981. *You Know: A Discourse-Functional Approach.* Amsterdam: John Benjamins.

Overstreet, Maryann, and George Yule. 1997a. "Locally Contingent Categorization in Discourse." *Discourse Processes* 23: 83–97.

———. 1997b. "On Being Inexplicit and Stuff in Contemporary American English." *Journal of English Linguistics* 25: 250–258.

———. 1999a. "Fostering L2 Pragmatic Awareness." *Applied Language Learning* 10: 1–14.

———. 1999b. "Formulaic Disclaimers." *Paper presented at the annual conference of the American Association for Applied Linguistics*, Stamford CT.

Palmer, Frank. 1986. *Mood and Modality.* Cambridge: Cambridge University Press.

Pawley, Andrew, and Florence Syder. 1983. "Two Puzzles for Linguistic Theory: Nativelike Selection and Nativelike Fluency." In *Language and Communication*, edited by J. Richards and R. Schmidt, 191–226. London: Longman.

Rips, L. J. 1989. "Similarity, Typicality, and Categorization." In *Similarity and Analogical Reasoning*, edited by S. Vosniadou and A. Ortony, 21–59. Cambridge: Cambridge University Press.

Romaine, Suzanne, and Deborah Lange. 1991. "The Use of *Like* as a Marker of Reported Speech and Thought: A Case of Grammaticalization in Progress." *American Speech* 66: 227–279.

Rommetveit, Ragnar. 1974. *On Message Structure.* London: John Wiley and Sons.

Rosch, Eleanor. 1974. "Linguistic Relativity." In *Human Communication: Theoretical Explorations*, edited by A. Silverstein, 95–121. Hillsdale, N. J.: Lawrence Erlbaum.

———. 1975a. "Cognitive Representations of Semantic Categories." *Journal of Experimental Psychology* 104: 192–233.

———. 1975b. "Cognitive Reference Points." *Cognitive Psychology* 7: 532-547.

———. 1977. "Human Categorization." In *Advances in Cross–Cultural Psychology*, edited by N. Warren. London: Academic Press.

———. 1978. "Principles of Categorization." In *Cognition and Categorization*, edited by E. Rosch, and B. Lloyd, 27-48. Hillsdale, N. J.: Lawrence Erlbaum.

Rosch, Eleanor, and C. B. Mervis. 1975. "Family Resemblances: Studies in the Internal Structure of Categories." *Cognitive Psychology* 8: 382–439.

Rosch, Eleanor, C. B. Mervis, W. D. Gray, D. M. Johnson, and P. Boyes-Bream. 1976. "Basic Objects in Natural Categories." *Cognitive Psychology* 2: 491–502.

Russell, Bertrand. 1905. "On Defining." *Mind* 14.

———. 1919. *Introduction to Mathematical Philosophy.* London: Allen and Unwin.

Sacks, Harvey. 1972. "On the Analyzability of Stories by Children." In *Directions in Sociolinguistics: The Ethnography of Communication*, edited by J. Gumperz, and D. Hymes, 325-345. New York: Holt, Rinehart and Winston.

———. 1992. *Lectures on Conversation*, Vol. 1. Cambridge: Blackwell.

Salinger, J. D. 1951. *The Catcher in the Rye*. Boston: Little, Brown.

Schank, Roger, and Robert Abelson. 1977. *Scripts, Plans, Goals, and Understanding*. Hillsdale, N. J.: Lawrence Erlbaum.

Schegloff, Emmanuel. 1992. "Repair after Next Turn: The Last Structurally-Provided Defense of Intersubjectivity in Conversation." *American Journal of Sociology* 97: 1295–1345.

Schegloff, Emmanuel, Gail Jefferson, and Harvey Sacks. 1977. "The Preference for Self-Correction in the Organization of Repair in Conversation." *Language* 53: 361–382.

Schiffrin, Deborah. 1987. *Discourse Markers*. Cambridge: Cambridge University Press.

———. 1990. "The Principle of Intersubjectivity in Conversation and Communication." *Semiotica* 80: 121–51.

———. 1994a. *Approaches to Discourse*. Oxford and Cambridge: Blackwell.

———. 1994b. "Making a List." *Discourse Processes* 17: 377–406.

Schutz, Alfred. 1932/1967. *The Phenomenology of the Social World*. Translated by G. Walsh and F. Lehnert. Evanston, Ill.: Northwestern University Press.

———. 1962. *Collected Papers* Vol. 1., edited by Arvid Broderson. The Hague: Martinus Nijhoff.

Schutz, Alfred, and Thomas Luckmann. 1977. *Strukturen der Lebenswelt*. Vol. 1. Frankfurt am Main: Suhrkamp.

———. 1984. *Strukturen der Lebenswelt*. Vol. 2. Frankfurt am Main: Suhrkamp.

Scollon, Ronald, and Suzanne B. K. Scollon. 1981. *Narrative, Literacy and Face in Interethnic Communication*. Norwood, NJ: Ablex Publishing Corporation.

———. 1983. "Face in Interethnic Communication." In *Language and Communication* , edited by J. C. Richards, and R. W. Schmidt. London: Longman.

Scott, Marvin, and Stanford Lyman. 1968. "Accounts." *American Sociological Review* 33: 46–62.

Sessums, Kevin. 1994. "Cruise Speed." *Vanity Fair*, Oct. 188-195, 270.

Shimron, Joseph, and Roberto Chernitsky. 1995. "Typicality Shift in Semantic Categories as a Result of Cultural Transition: Evidence from Jewish Argentine Immigrants in Israel." *Discourse Processes* 19: 265–78.

Smith, Edward E., and Douglas Medin. 1981. *Categories and Concepts*. Cambridge, Mass.: MIT Press.

Smith, Edward E., E. Shoben, and J. Rips. 1974. "Structure and Processes in Semantic Memory: A Featural Model for Semantic Decisions." *Psychological Review* 81: 214–41.

Spaulding, Thomas, and Gregory Murphy. 1996. "Effects of Background Knowledge on Category Construction." *Journal of Experimental Psychology* 22: 525–538.

Sperber, Dan, and Deirdre Wilson. 1995. *Relevance*. Oxford: Basil Blackwell.

Stevenson, Marjolyn. 1987. *English Syntax*. Boston: Little, Brown.

Svartvik, Jan, and Randolph Quirk. 1980. *A Corpus of English Conversation.* Lund, Sweden: Gleerup.

Tannen, Deborah (ed.). 1982. *Spoken and Written Language: Exploring Orality and Literacy.* Norwood, N.J.: Ablex.

———. 1984. *Conversational Style.* Norwood, NJ: Ablex.

———. 1989. *Talking Voices: Repetition, Dialogue and Imagery in Conversational Discourse.* Cambridge: Cambridge University Press.

Taylor, John. 1995. *Linguistic Categorization.* Oxford: Oxford University Press.

Tsohatzidis, Savas (ed.). 1990. *Meanings and Prototypes.* London and New York: Routledge.

Tsui, Amy B. M. 1994. *English Conversation.* Oxford: Oxford University Press.

Turque, Bill, Mark Miller, and Andrew Murr. 1994. "New Twists in the Simpson Case." *Newsweek* 4 July, 22–33.

Tversky, A. 1977. "Features of Similarity." *Psychological Review* 84: 327-352.

van Mechelen, Ivan, J. Hampton, R. Michalski, and P. Theus (eds.). 1993. *Categories and Concepts.* London: Academic Press.

Vygotsky, Lev S. 1962. *Thought and language.* Cambridge, Mass.: MIT Press.

Ward, Gregory, and Betty Birner. 1993. "The Semantics and Pragmatics of 'and everything.'" *Journal of Pragmatics* 19: 205–214.

Welsh, Irvine. 1994. *The Acid House.* London: Vintage.

Widdowson, Henry. 1996. *Linguistics.* Oxford: Oxford University Press.

Wittgenstein, Ludwig. 1953. *Philosophical Investigations.* Translated by G. E. M. Anscombe. New York: Macmillan.

Wong Fillmore, Lily. 1994. "The Role and Function of Formulaic Speech in Conversation." In *What's Going On Here?*, edited by A. Grimshaw, 230–269. Norwood, N.J.: Ablex.

Yamanaka, Lois-Ann. 1996. *Wild Meat and the Bully Burgers.* New York: Farrar, Straus and Giroux.

Yule, George. 1996. *Pragmatics.* Oxford: Oxford University Press.

———. 1998. *Explaining English Grammar.* Oxford: Oxford University Press.

Zadeh, Lofti. 1965. "Fuzzy Sets." *Information and Control* 8: 338–353.

Ziff, Paul. 1972. *Understanding Understanding.* Ithaca, N. Y.: Cornell University Press.

Zipf, George. 1949. *Human Behavior and the Principle of Least Effort.* Cambridge, Mass.: Addison-Wesley.

Index

Printed in the United States
21524LVS00001B/87